The Art and Science of Classroom Assessment
The Missing Part of Pedagogy

Susan M. Brookhart

ASHE-ERIC Higher Education Report Volume 27, Number 1

Prepared by

ERIC Clearinghouse on Higher Education
The George Washington University
URL: www.eriche.org

In cooperation with

Association for the Study
of Higher Education
URL: http://www.tiger.coe.missouri.edu/~ashe

Published by

Graduate School of Education and Human Development
The George Washington University
URL: www.gwu.edu

Adrianna J. Kezar, Series Editor

Cite as

Brookhart, S. M. (1999). *The Art and Science of Classroom Assessment: The Missing Part of Pedagogy.* ASHE-ERIC Higher Education Report (Vol. 27, No. 1). Washington, DC: The George Washington University, Graduate School of Education and Human Development.

Library of Congress Catalog Card Number 99-63955
ISSN 0884-0040
ISBN 1-878380-89-3

Managing Editor: Lynne J. Scott
Manuscript Editor: Barbara M. Fishel
Cover Design by Michael David Brown, Inc., The Red Door
Gallery, Rockport, ME

The ERIC Clearinghouse on Higher Education invites individuals to submit proposals for writing monographs for the *ASHE-ERIC Higher Education Report* series. Proposals must include:
1. A detailed manuscript proposal of not more than five pages.
2. A chapter-by-chapter outline.
3. A 75-word summary to be used by several review committees for the initial screening and rating of each proposal.
4. A vita and a writing sample.

ERIC Clearinghouse on Higher Education
Graduate School of Education and Human Development
The George Washington University
One Dupont Circle, Suite 630
Washington, DC 20036-1183

This publication was prepared partially with funding from the Office of Educational Research and Improvement, U.S. Department of Education, under contract no. ED-99-00-0036. The opinions expressed in this report do not necessarily reflect the positions or policies of OERI or the Department.

EXECUTIVE SUMMARY

How does an instructor know whether students are learning what the instructor is trying to teach them? How do students find out how they are doing, and can they use that information to study more effectively? Would students be able to tell what the instructor thinks is important for them to learn by looking at the assignments that "count" in a course? Good assessment yields good information about the results of instruction; it is itself a necessary component of good instruction. Students who do not understand what they are aiming to know and how they will be expected to demonstrate their achievements will not be able to participate fully in managing their own learning. Sound assessment and grading practices help teachers improve their own instruction, improve students' motivation, focus students' effort, and increase students' achievement.

"Assessment" means to gather and interpret information about students' achievement, and "achievement" means the level of attainment of learning goals of college courses. Assessing students' achievement is generally accomplished through tests, classroom and take-home assignments, and assigned projects. Strictly speaking, "assessment" refers to assignments and tasks that provide information, and "evaluation" refers to judgments based on that information.

Why Is Classroom Assessment of Students' Achievement Important?

Students should be able to tell what the instructor thinks is important for them to learn by looking at a course's tests, projects, and other assignments. These assessments are an instructor's way of gathering information about what students have learned, and they can then use them to make important decisions—about students' grades, the content of future lessons, the revision of the structure or content of a course or program. Thus, it is important that student assessments in higher education classes give dependable information.

How Can an Instructor Ensure the Quality of Information From Classroom Assessments?

Information from classroom assessments—grades, scores, and judgments about students' work resulting from tests, assignments, projects, and other work—must be meaningful and accurate (that is, valid and reliable). The results of assessment should be indicators of the particular learning goals for the course, measuring those goals in proportion to their emphasis in the course. An instructor should be confident that students' scores accurately represent their level of achievement.

The Art and Science of Classroom Assessment describes five different kinds of learning goals or "achievement targets": knowledge of facts and concepts (recall); thinking, reasoning, and problem solving using one's knowledge; skill in procedures or processes, such as using a microscope; constructing projects, reports, artwork, or other products; and dispositions, such as appreciating the importance of a discipline. Different methods of assessment are better suited for measuring different kinds of achievement.

What Methods of Assessment Are Particularly Suited to Various Achievement Targets, and How Are They Constructed, Administered, and Scored?

Four basic methods of assessment are presented: paper-and-pencil tests, performance assessments, oral questions, and portfolios. Paper-and-pencil tests are the most commonly used form of assessment in higher education. Performance assessments are tasks and associated scoring schemes ("rubrics") that require students to make or do something whose quality can be observed and judged. Oral questions are commonly asked in the context of classroom discussions, more often in smaller seminar-style classes than in large lecture sections. Portfolios are collections of students' work over time, according to some purpose and guiding principles; they usually include students' reflection on the work. *The Art and Science of Classroom Assessment* provides suggestions about writing good tests, performance tasks, oral questions, and portfolio specifications, and about constructing scoring schemes that examine performance according to learning goals. Two kinds of scoring—objective, requiring a right/ wrong or yes/no decision, and subjective, requiring judgments of quality along a continuum—and principles for devising scoring schemes and examples are described.

How Can the Results of Several Assessments Be Meaningfully Combined Into One Composite Grade?

Grading usually requires constructing one score or judgment from several scores on various assignments and tests. The combination must be valid and appropriately weight the scores of various components according to their places in the instructor's intentions for the course. A set of good assessments can be rendered into an invalid grade if the individual scores are not carefully combined. Four methods of determining final grades serve different grading purposes an instructor might intend, depending on the course: the median method, weighted letter grades, total possible points, and holistic rating.

The topic of grading is found in the higher education literature, largely under discussions or studies of "grade inflation." A review of the recent literature on grade inflation may yield some surprises for readers. Although grade inflation is a concern at the present time, previously during this century writers expressed some concern about grade *deflation*. Several authors have raised related issues that suggest the topic is more multifaceted than the straight-line function the term "inflation" implies: issues about the nature of education, differences in grades among the disciplines, and the noncomparability of grades in different historical periods.

In What Areas Might Faculty Improve Their Assessment Skills, and What Resources Are Available to Help?

Assessment of students' work in higher education classrooms is important—and important to do well. One science professor has been heard to comment that professors sometimes measure the specimens in their labs more accurately than they measure the students in their classrooms, yet important human consequences follow from both. Faculty members who wish to improve their skills in assessment can find some good resources already available, some of the best of which are recent books and articles, and easily obtained materials on the Internet. *The Art and Science of Classroom Assessment* summarizes some of what the author thinks are the best "next step" resources for readers.

What Conclusions Can Be Drawn From the Review of the Literature?

The literature on principles of classroom assessment has been written mostly for K–12 education. *The Art and Science of Classroom Assessment* uses examples and discusses assessment contexts relevant to college courses and young (and not-so-young) adult students. Empirical studies of classroom assessment in higher education underscore the importance of instructors' fairness, clarity in tests, assignments, and scoring, and clear descriptions of the achievement target or learning goal in higher education classrooms. More studies are needed that investigate the needs, types, results, and effectiveness of assessment in higher education and that tie the findings to theories about adult learners. Some excellent resources presently exist for helping instructors design and conduct valid, reliable, fair, and interesting assessments of students' work—a crucial function in higher education classrooms.

CONTENTS

Tables

FOREWORD

In her opening address to the Association for the Study of Higher Education in 1998, Yvonna Lincoln encouraged higher education professionals to embrace an ethic of love in their research, teaching, service, and administrative responsibilities. This ethic can help us to conduct our activities in ways that are fair, equitable, and compassionate. One illustration of this ethic is to provide students with detailed feedback and assessment of their work, even though it can be time consuming and difficult, with few rewards. The benefit for students and learning can be significant.

One argument for the value of classroom assessment of students is that an instructor can know whether students are learning what the instructor is trying to teach them, and students can find out how they are doing and then use that information to study more effectively. Good teachers care about these issues, and state legislatures, education commissions, coordinating boards, trustees, and others are calling for assessment of students' learning. Administrators are paying closer attention to faculty members' assessment of students; program and college procedures are being established. But one of the most compelling arguments for the need to improve faculty members' classroom assessment is that it helps to improve students' learning! More and more studies demonstrate that students who participated in a class where grading was based on performance increased their competency.

Susan M. Brookhart, associate professor of education at Duquesne University, has written a compelling description of effective assessment of students' achievement in college and university classes. She describes the importance of learning goals or achievement targets as a necessary first step toward classroom assessment and reminds us that assessment should be planned at the same time the syllabus is prepared. One of the most important principles of *The Art and Science of Classroom Assessment* is that assessment is part of effective instruction. It is a *necessary* part of planning/instruction/assessment. Brookhart clearly defines terms and shows how to use them through examples, summarizes the literature on classroom assessment in higher education, details methods of assessment, delineates the development of good assessment instruments and scoring procedures, reviews grading strategies, and provides several models for achieving the goal of quality classroom assessment and resources for faculty to improve assessment skills. A quality product results if the feedback is valid and reliable. *The Art and Science of Classroom Assessment* provides the needed evidence, resources, and advice to guide new and experienced faculty members, including many informative tables with concrete examples.

The Art and Science of Classroom Assessment provides insights into three areas challenging the academy: (a) professional standards of assessment; (b) outcomes assessment; and (c) grade inflation. No professional standards exist for assessment of students in higher education, and it is hoped this book will help to establish a set of standards for faculty members to follow and to model for graduate students, our future teachers. Perhaps it can begin a dialogue about developing a set of standards for assessing students' work. Brookhart notes that classroom assessment needs to be linked to institutional and state assessment of student outcomes, especially given that accreditors and state legislatures are requiring proof of students' learning before allocating funds. With regard to the issue of grade inflation and grading policies, the rise in the average grades of students in college is an issue of accountability that should be addressed. In an increasingly litigious society, grading policies are becoming increasingly important.

Several other ASHE-ERIC Higher Education Reports provide additional perspectives on assessment. Karen and Karl Schilling's *Proclaiming and Sustaining Excellence* (vol. 26, no. 3) provides an overview of the assessment movement and its impact on the academy, and examines important issues for chairs and deans. Elizabeth Creamer's *Assessing Faculty Publication Productivity* (vol. 26, no. 2) addresses the assessment of faculty. Mimi Wolverton's *A New Alliance: Continuous Quality and Classroom Effectiveness* (vol. 23, no. 6) examines seven institutions' use of the Malcolm Baldrige standards for increasing effectiveness in the classroom. And Lion Gardiner's *Redesigning Higher Education: Producing Dramatic Gains in Student Learning* (vol. 23, no. 7) details how assessment can improve students' learning.

It is hoped that *The Art and Science of Classroom Assessment* will provide the inspiration and guidance faculty need to assess students' work accurately and fairly.

Adrianna J. Kezar
Series Editor,
Assistant Professor of Higher Education, and
Director, ERIC Clearinghouse on Higher Education

INTRODUCTION

The Purpose of Assessing Students

How does an instructor know whether students are learning what he or she is trying to teach them? How do students find out how they are doing, and can they use that information to study more effectively? Can students tell what the instructor thinks is important for them to learn by looking at the assignments that "count" in a course? Good teachers care about such questions. Sound assessment and grading practices help teachers improve students' motivation, effort, and achievement. Sound assessment makes it easier to design and deliver good instruction and to describe its results.

"Assessment" is defined here as gathering and interpreting information about student achievement; "student achievement" is defined as level of attainment of learning goals in college courses, and its assessment is generally accomplished through tests, classroom and take-home assignments, and projects that students undertake to provide information about what they are learning. Strictly speaking, "assessment" refers to assignments and tasks that provide information, and "evaluation" refers to judgments based on that information.

The need for quality information in student assessment

Assessing students' achievement in higher education classrooms provides vital information for several different purposes. It provides feedback to students that fosters learning and provides information to the professor about students' achievement of learning goals for the course. Assessment provides the basis for students' grades for a course, which in turn seriously affect students' progress through higher education, future course selections, and vocational and avocational choices. It provides the basis for instructors' evaluation and adjustment of their own teaching. Assessment by students of a course can be part of the evaluative information considered by the program of which the course is a component. Because important decisions are based on information derived from classroom assessments, it is imperative that the information be of high quality: accurate, dependable, meaningful, and appropriate.

This monograph is about assessing students' achievement in college and university classes. It is not about university outcomes assessment or program evaluation, although both of these purposes depend on regular, well-done classroom assessment. It is written primarily for college and university faculty, but a secondary audience would include college and university administrators, who may find that knowledge of this topic will help them deal with questions or problems their faculty or students may have. This monograph will answer several questions:

1. Why is classroom assessment of students' achievement of course learning goals important?
2. How can one ensure the quality of information derived from classroom assessment?
3. What assessment methods are particularly suited to various targets, both in general and in academic disciplines? How are they constructed, administered, and scored?
4. How can the results of several different assessments be meaningfully combined into one composite course grade for a student?
5. In what areas might faculty members improve their assessment skills, and what resources are available to them for doing so?

Assessment as part of a model of instruction
Assessment is generally considered one of three aspects of instruction (along with planning and teaching). Many different theorists and practitioners of instruction have described models of instruction (see, e.g., Kubiszyn & Borich, 1993). Most have a similar, three-part construction. Sometimes the model is linear: Planning informs instruction informs assessment. But that description is overly simplistic, and a more accurate way of thinking about teaching would involve a set of bidirectional relationships. Planning and decisions about what students should learn inform choices about what kinds of instructional activities will help students learn the particular knowledge, skills, thinking and reasoning strategies, and so on. But the availability of certain instructional activities, for example, the existence of a good film or a well-tested exercise on a certain topic, sometimes informs planning. Planning decisions about what students are to learn should inform assessment, but sometimes the results of assessments describe students' knowledge in progress and result in changing plans, for example, to reteach material that was not learned. Assessment can and should be integrated with instruction and should inform both instruction and ongoing course planning.

This report illustrates how this relationship can happen when assessments are valid and reliable, that is, when they give appropriate, meaningful, and accurate information.

The classroom assessment environment

The way an instructor approaches assessment affects the way students perceive a class, the material for study, and their own work (Brookhart, 1997; Rodabaugh & Kravitz, 1994; Stiggins & Conklin, 1992). Eight aspects of the classroom assessment environment have been identified, based on research in public school classrooms: purposes of assessment, methods of assessment, selection criteria, quality of assessment, feedback, the teacher's characteristics, students' perceptions, and the policies for assessment under which teachers work (Stiggins & Conklin, 1992).

The idea of a classroom assessment environment is important because it focuses instructors on the impact of their approaches to assessment on students' motivation and achievement. Table 1 presents interview questions from a study of the assessment environment in college classrooms (Brookhart, 1997), which is useful for readers' reflection on their own approaches to assessment as they begin to read this monograph.

Organization of This Monograph
Principles of educational assessment

This monograph summarizes work in educational measurement and instruction, which together suggest principles for classroom assessment that enhances instruction and produces meaningful information about students' achievement. The principles draw on theoretical and empirical work broadly applicable to all levels of learning. The aim of the next six sections is to present a readable summary of these principles, enough for a good orientation to classroom assessment in higher education, but not enough to substitute for a thorough study of educational measurement. (Readers who wish to pursue the topic of student assessment in higher education will find resources listed in the last section.)

Student assessment should be multidimensional, and it should be the focus of ongoing communication with students about their achievement of the course's objectives. The methodology for classroom assessment can be thought of as a toolkit that faculty use for accomplishing their pur-

TABLE 1

Questions for Instructors' Reflection on Assessment

1. For what purposes do you use assessment? (grades, grouping, diagnosis, motivation, evaluation of instruction, communicating expectations, planning instruction)

2. What types of assessment methods do you use? (tests, quizzes, performance assessments, oral questioning, assignments, student peer ratings, self-ratings)

   • In what proportion do you use these assessments?

   • What kinds of performance do you assess? (recall, analysis, comparison, inference, evaluation)

   • How do you deal with cheating?

   • Do you assess students' dispositions as well as achievement? (motivation, interest, maturity, study skills) Formally or informally?

3. What criteria do you use to select an assessment? (results fit purpose, method matches instruction, ease of development, ease of use, ease of scoring, origin of assessment, time required, degree of objectivity, thinking skills tapped, effective control of cheating)

4. How would you judge the quality of your assessments for giving you the information you need about students' achievement?

5. How do you give feedback to students about their performance? (written, oral, grades, informal)

6. How do you view the role of teacher? (knowledge presenter, facilitator of student-constructed learning) How do you view the role of student? (cooperative, competitive) How much of students' failure or success do you attribute to the student? To the teacher?

7. How do you view the characteristics of the students in your class(es)? (ability, work habits, maturity, social skills, willingness to perform, need for feedback, self-assessment skills, sense of fairness, reaction to testing/assessment, expectations of the teacher)

8. Are there assessment policies you must follow? Describe them.

poses. This report presents such a toolkit, organized according to a modified version of a framework for understanding types of classroom assessment (see Stiggins, 1992, 1997).

Assessment methods can be grouped into four general categories: paper-and-pencil tests, performance assessments of processes or products, oral communication, and portfolios. For each category, objective (right/wrong or present/absent) and subjective (judgment of degree of quality) scoring can be developed. Different assessments are necessary to cover the full range of achievement targets: knowledge, thinking, processes, products, and dispositions.

Review of higher education literature

Although student assessment in higher education should be informed by general principles of assessment and instruction, some features of higher education make it a special context for classroom assessment: widely varying class sizes, the noncompulsory nature of enrollment, the possibility of a grade of Incomplete, and the fact that students are adults. This report also presents a review of literature specific to student assessment in higher education, including some general essays and studies ("Defining Student Learning for Assessment"), some discipline-specific literature ("Assessment in the Disciplines"), and some literature on grading in higher education ("Grade Distributions and Grading Policies").

The author, with the help of the staff of the ERIC Clearinghouse on Higher Education, reviewed the literature on assessment in higher education classes by first searching the ERIC database for materials from 1985 to the present that included the phrase "classroom assessment" in the title, abstract, or descriptor and "higher education," "colleges," or "universities" in the descriptor. The search identified resources about student assessment in higher education classes. Two categories of literature resulting from the search were set aside because the focus of this report is assessment of students' achievement of learning goals for the course: (a) resources that were basically about program evaluation or outcomes assessment, where the interest was in aggregated group achievement for institutional purposes; and (b) resources about classroom assessment techniques (see Angelo & Cross, 1993; K. Cross & Angelo, 1988), where assessment is anonymous and the unit of analysis is the class, not individual students. The assessment of students' achievement can be formative and not included in the course grade, or official and summative, counting in a course grade, but the individual student's name is known and individual progress or achievement is the concern.

Some sources identified by hand were added to the literature on student assessment from the ERIC review. Recent issues of *Journal on Excellence in College Teaching* and *College Teaching* and recent issues of discipline-specific journals from professional organizations of teachers, such as *Journal of College Science Teaching* and *College English,* were examined. A search of Dissertation Abstracts International yielded one useful recent reference. The reference lists in some of the articles identified additional useful sources.

Professional Standards for Student Assessment

Professional standards for teachers' competency in classroom assessment exist for K–12 teachers (American Federation, 1990; Joint Advisory Committee, 1993). Their content provides a useful springboard for discussing both professional competence and fairness in assessment in higher education. *Standards for Teacher Competence in Educational Assessment of Students* (American Federation, 1990) states that teachers should be skilled in choosing and developing assessment methods appropriate for instructional decisions; administering, scoring, and interpreting the results of assessments; using assessment results when making decisions about individual students, planning teaching, developing the curriculum, and improving programs; developing valid grading procedures based on assessments of students; communicating the results of assessment; and recognizing unethical, illegal, and inappropriate methods and uses of information about assessment. Some discipline-specific professional standards also exist for K–12 teachers (e.g., National Council, 1989) that are applicable for the college level.

The Joint Committee on Standards, sponsored by 16 professional educational organizations spanning elementary through postsecondary levels, is preparing Standards for Evaluation of Students, to be ready about 2002. These standards are grouped into four categories: proprietary, utility, accuracy, and fairness. The proprietary standards state that evaluations of students should be conducted according to sound educational principles and meet the educational and informational needs of students as well as their instructors and institutions (Joint Committee, 1998). Further, they call for formal, written policies and procedures for evaluating students. The other three categories of standards—utility (or practicality and usability), accuracy, and fairness—also contribute to sound assessment in postsecondary education. Readers who ground their assessments in the principles described in this report will be aligning their practice of assessment with professional standards.

DEFINING STUDENT LEARNING
FOR ASSESSMENT

The goals for learning in an academic course should be specified from the outset, and then those goals should be the focus of student assessment. Whether the instructor calls them "course objectives," "goals," or something else, every instructor should be able to articulate what he or she intends students to learn (Walvoord & Anderson, 1998). Sometimes, for example, for an introductory or survey course, those goals will be very structured and centered on comprehension and application of basic concepts. Sometimes, as for an advanced seminar, those goals will be broad. For example, the goals for a senior seminar in educational psychology might be for the student to read and understand literature in an area he or she chooses within the broad domains of either cognition or motivation. But the instructor still must specify what the student is meant to accomplish and then assess to what extent that happens. In this example, the instructor would need to find ways to decide whether and how well a student had selected, read, and understood an appropriate body of literature.

College instructors have been known to comment on what they might term the restrictive nature of such "outcomes driven" instruction that does not leave room for "creativity." This approach represents a narrower interpretation of the terms "objectives" and "goals" than is helpful. The existence of intentions for instruction does not mean that students' original thought is precluded; original application of ideas may well be considered one of the instructional aims for a course.

Some instructors are used to focusing on content when planning a course. They are more likely to ask themselves "What material should I present?" than "What do I want my students to learn?" This approach makes assessment difficult. Worse, it changes the focus of teaching and learning from one in which intentional learning is expected of students and facilitation of that learning (including, but not limited to, presenting material) is expected of the instructor, to one in which "receiving" material is expected of the students. After they have received the material presented, the students must figure out what to do with it. Students are out of luck if at exam time their answers to a question do not match the instructor's take on it.

Many professors who think in terms of presenting material really do have a set of concepts they want their students to understand in certain ways, and they can express their intentions for their course in the form of goals or objectives if they stop and think about it. The message of this report on assessment is that this is a good thing to do! Put those goals in the syllabus, share them with students, and then make sure that their learning experiences and assessments match them. Doing so does not make the material any easier (although it should make the course a little "easier" for the students to deal with); it doesn't "give away the farm." But it does keep everyone, both instructor and students, focused on what is important to learn. It gives purpose to class activities, assignments, and assessments. When students understand the purpose behind an assessment, even a difficult one, they are less likely to complain, more likely to tackle it sincerely, and more likely to learn from it (Covington, 1992).

In this report, the terms "instructional objectives," "learning goals," and "achievement targets" are used interchangeably to mean the instructor's intentions for students' learning of course material. Some writers use the term "goals" for relatively broad learning intentions and "objectives" for more specific ones. Because this report is aimed toward a broad range of postsecondary instructors and their courses, general use of these terms is appropriate. What is a broad goal in one course may be a more specific objective in another context. Learning objectives or goals have been characterized as "achievement targets" (Stiggins, 1992, 1997). This metaphor is an apt one, because it captures how it feels to be a student "shooting for" something, with all its connotations of effort, care, and aim, and it also captures something of the "prize" of learning, of hitting the bull's-eye.

Kinds of Achievement Targets

Achievement targets come in several varieties, described as knowledge, thinking, products, skills, and dispositions (Stiggins, 1997). Most college courses have achievement targets in several of these categories. Some assessments are more effective than others for gathering information about students' learning in a particular category.

Knowledge of facts and concepts is basic to most college learning. For example, it may be important for students in an algebra course to know that the point of intersection of lines charting the profitability functions of two choices in a business venture is the point at which both choices would yield the same profit. In a European history course, it may be important for students to know that Hitler was the dictator of Germany from 1934 to 1945 (fact) or that his ascendancy may be explained by the theory that a "power vacuum" existed in Germany at a time of deep economic distress (concept).

In this information age, an interesting phenomenon is occurring with regard to knowledge of facts and concepts. There are way too many facts to remember, and some of a good education consists of knowing which facts and concepts are important to commit to memory, available for instant retrieval any time, and which facts and concepts are best "memorized" by knowing where to look for them in books, computer files, or other resources. Learning what is acceptable to "forget" and learning how to let go of that material is a skill students' grandparents did not need as much as today's students do.

Assessment of students' knowledge of facts and concepts is probably the most straightforward, and certainly the most common, form of assessment in college courses. The current trumpeting about "higher order thinking," important though it is, should not be read to mean that knowledge of facts and concepts is not important. It means a balance must be achieved in teaching knowledge, skills needed to obtain more knowledge, and strategies or methods for constructing new knowledge.

Thinking, understanding, and applying concepts, sometimes called "higher order thinking," also form part of the learning goals for most college courses. It is not enough to know and be able to recognize or even recall a fact unless one knows what to do with that fact once it is retrieved from memory or from resource material. Thoughtful application of concepts learned has long been a goal of higher education and, indeed, is a traditional hallmark of an educated person.

Students who understand concepts can use them to reason, argue, persuade, explain, illustrate, and discuss a variety of statements, scenarios, points of view, and the like. Students who understand concepts can use them to solve novel problems. For assessment, it is important to emphasize that a student is not demonstrating understanding if the problem is not new to the student. If a chemical reaction problem on a chemistry exam is the same as one that was worked in class, the task is one of recall, no matter how difficult a recall task it may be. If the chemistry professor wants to assess whether students can use principles they learned about how chemical

For assessment, it is important to emphasize that a student is not demonstrating understanding if the problem is not new to the student.

reactions occur to solve a chemical reaction problem, the problem has to be one the students have not seen before and one that can be solved by applying the particular principles the instructor intends to assess. (See "Options for Classroom Assessment" for a more detailed discussion of this principle.)

Sometimes learning goals for students result in the production of academic *products*. A student in a creative writing class who produces a short story, a student in a biology lab who produces a project and a lab report, and a student in a history class who produces a videotape all share with the art student in the studio the characteristic that the major demonstration of their achievement is a product. Products vary in quality, and this quality can be judged—by the instructor, other students, and professionals—according to agreed-upon criteria.

Some learning goals for students include assessment of procedural *skills*. Some areas more than others require the intentional teaching, learning, and assessing of skills, but all academic areas require the acquisition of skills. Biology students must learn how to use laboratory equipment safely, effectively, and with skill. Computer students must learn how to use keyboards, mice, and software. Math students must learn how to use graphing calculators. Social science students must learn how to use various kinds of maps. Nursing students must learn how to use hypodermic needles to give injections and sphygmomanometers to measure blood pressure. All students must learn how to use the library to find information. On and on the list goes.

If procedural skills are an important part of learning goals for a course, the level of skill that a student has acquired must be assessed. Often, it can be done by performance assessment, in which the instructor or other students observe the student's performance of a particular skill or set of skills on a task and rate, judge, or even describe in words the quality of the performance they have observed.

Knowledge, thinking, products, and skills are the academic learning goals for most courses. *Dispositions* and interests are intended, if unstated, learning goals for many courses as well. For example, most instructors hope that their students develop an appreciation for the importance of their field and its contribution to humanity. Most instructors also harbor the hope that some of their students will develop a personal interest in their field, pursuing it further in their education and perhaps as their vocational choice.

Most times, it is best that these dispositional learning goals, stated or not, not be assessed for inclusion in a course grade. After all, if a student knows that the "right" answer to the question "Are you interested in math?" is "Yes, very" and that that answer will earn an A, then all of a sudden many students will register interest! But it is reasonable, without the consequences of a grade attached, to assess students' dispositions toward things that matter to the conduct of the class. The options for assessment described later include methods of assessing dispositions and interests as well as more academic targets.

ERIC Resources

Tables 2 and 3 summarize ERIC resources about the assessment of students in higher education (but not about grading, which is covered in "Grade Distributions and Grading Policies"). Table 2 lists essays and descriptions about classroom assessment in higher education; Table 3 lists empirical studies about classroom assessment in higher education.

Many of the essays and descriptions in Table 2 are general guidelines for planning assessment (S. Brown, Rust, & Gibbs, 1994; Community College of Vermont, 1992; Lantos, 1992; McTighe & Ferrara, 1994; Wergin, 1988). A theme they share is that assessment should be planned at the same time the syllabus is prepared. The first step in planning a course is to identify its purpose and the learning goals and intentions for students. The syllabus, assigned readings, plans for individual classes and lessons, tests, papers, and projects and other assignments should all relate to the learning intended for the course. This step is obvious when declarative knowledge is involved, when mastery of a body of concepts, facts, and generalizations is the goal for students. But the same principle applies when procedural knowledge (e.g., how to conduct historical research or perform laboratory experiments) or critical thinking and reasoning form part of the learning goals. The kinds of goals selected for a course have implications for the instruction and assessment that should go on, but the principle that goals, instruction, and assessment are related still holds.

Some of the articles describe specific methods of assessment, their purposes and uses. Portfolios (Crouch & Fontaine, 1994; Glasgow, 1993) are a method that has long been used in the fine arts; other disciplines, most notably writing, are experimenting with this assessment format today. Tests

TABLE 2

Essays About and Descriptions of Classroom Assessment In College and University Classrooms

Source	Topic	Main points
S. Brown, Rust, & Gibbs, 1994	For faculty development in assessment	• Clear treatment with many examples of methods of assessment in higher education
Buchanan & Rogers, 1990	Suggestions for dealing with classes of more than 80 with regard to essay testing, makeup exams, and writing new exam questions	• Cafeteria approach, in which students can decide to take essay or objective final, depending on average beforehand. Only 6-7 students in 300 end up taking an essay final. • No makeups: students may drop lowest exam grade or drop the zero for a missed exam. • Student-generated test items tend to be conceptual and at least as good as textbook test-bank items but also cover class material.
Community College of Vermont, 1992	Course planning	• Part 3 describes how to plan a syllabus, instruction, and evaluation. • Recommends clear course objectives • Recommends criterion-referenced grading
Crouch & Fontaine, 1994	Portfolios	• Portfolio assessment changes the way students think about writing and write. • Describes portfolio use in a developmental writing program • Portfolios stress "reworking, rethinking, and revising." • Assignments put in portfolio are not judged summatively until the end of the semester, so there is room for trial and improvement.
Glasgow, 1993	Portfolios in a developmental writing course	• Students became more reflective and confident about their reading and writing. • Gives objectives on the syllabus and describes students' work on each one • Literacy autobiographies describe a student's history as a writer, shared in reader response groups; oral and written responses, rewriting; focused correction from instructor • Grades based on papers plus "risk taking, changing, practicing writing, and peer editing"
Hackett & Levine, 1993	Assessment methods	• Symposium, oral exam, writing, journals, portfolios, and other specific suggestions

Source	Topic	Main points
Harris, 1994	Multicultural concerns in classroom assessment	• Cultural concerns that get in the way of conventional college assessment include taboos against eye contact (as lacking respect for authority), competing, or standing out; values and experience with hands-on as opposed to abstract learning; oral as opposed to silent learning • Suggests using assessment techniques that build on those issues: peer feedback, learning logs (academic journals), learning file, minicapstone experiences (students reflect on any final assignment, what they learned, and what it means to them)
Lantos, 1992	Expectations for written work should be "clear, demanding, positive, and enthusiastically held" to motivate students' writing	• Put general requirements in syllabus, specific requirements in an assignment sheet for each assignment; make a criterion list and spell out attributes of each criterion; use the criteria when grading the work; return work promptly
McClymer & Knoles, 1992	Much of what students are asked to do on tests calls upon learning facts and strategies but not on understanding	• Uses Perkins's "thinking frames" (information, problem solving, epistemology, and inquiry) to describe academic thinking • Questions that allow students to approach a problem-solving task as an informational one encourage ersatz learning. • Acritical student coping mechanisms include clumps (amassing elements of critical analysis minus their logic—data packing, jargon packing, assertion packing) and shapes (using the logical forms of critical analysis without substance—borrowed analysis, surface analysis, or insistence upon a single thread of meaning), which can allow students to pass courses without mastering their meaning. Suggested solution is authentic testing. • We ask too much of students by giving them unauthentic questions to answer, implying there is a closure and right answer, and then ask too little by comments that tell them they are successful or partially successful if they use clumps or shapes.

TABLE 2 (continued)

Source	Topic	Main points
McTighe & Ferrara, 1994	Classroom assessment	• A primer of classroom assessment principles and methods for all levels from preschool to graduate school • Primary purpose of classroom assessment is to improve students' learning and inform learning. • Use multiple sources of information to assess learning. • Assure validity, reliability, and fairness in assessment. • Base assessment on intended learning outcomes and purpose, and audience for information.
Murray, 1990	Tests should be learning opportunities	• Various methods of using tests to teach are presented (some more valid than others): second-chance exams and grade algorithms, "brain-buster" exams to be done by groups, group multiple-choice tests, peer-mediated testing, paired testing, answer justification, take-home exams, immediate feedback, cost/benefit testing, alternate-forms retesting, and reaction or opinion papers.
O'Keefe, 1996	Grades should be based on substantive comments on work	• Turnaround time is important, but so are critical comments. • Experience with standard assignments (the example is a marketing case report) leads instructors to be able to anticipate most comments. • Sheets with numbered comment codes save time and let students see their comments.
Wergin, 1988	Classroom assessment	• A short primer on classroom assessment • Relevance versus control in assessment • Item writing for classroom tests • Validity and reliability

(Buchanan & Rogers, 1990; McClymer & Knoles, 1992; Murray, 1990) are an efficient way to gather information about students' knowledge of facts, concepts, and generalizations, and at least a limited amount of information about how students can use those concepts to reason or solve problems.

Tests are almost a necessity in very large classes, which can range from 80 or so students to several hundred (Buchanan & Rogers, 1990). Large introductory survey classes commonly include knowledge of a body of facts and concepts as important learning goals, and tests are an efficient use of assessment time for these classes. It is still important to make these classes as interactive as possible and to develop students' thinking skills (Walvoord & Anderson, 1998).

A variety of activities can be used to assess students' achievement of learning goals: symposia, oral exams, journals, papers, and other activities (Hackett & Levine, 1993). The key is not to use novelty for its own sake in assessing students but to ask of any task or activity that students might undertake what knowledge and skills the assignment would tap; what information about students' achievement of the course's learning goals would be available from their performance on the assignment; and what knowledge, skills, and understanding could not be assessed effectively using the method. Activities can often become learning experiences in their own right, serving double duty: Students learn from doing them, and the instructor learns about what students know and can do by reviewing them. Assessment and instruction are both served.

Table 3 presents empirical studies of assessment of students in higher education. In general, these studies confirm and emphasize that the principles of good instruction and assessment are effective and have desired results when implemented in college classrooms. Students do not like norm-referenced grading in which their performances are compared with their peers. Rather, they prefer that their work be compared with a criterion or standard of quality, and they do better work under those circumstances (Jacobsen, 1993; O'Sullivan & Johnson, 1993). Students appreciate opportunities to work together on evaluations (Stearns, 1996), not least because their scores are higher when they do. Unfortunately, at least one survey (Guthrie, 1992) found that at three institutions—a research university, a comprehensive college, and a liberal arts college—many of the assessments used in courses tapped lower order cognition, such as recall of facts and concepts, not the higher order thinking for which the institutions were noted.

An interesting series of simulation studies based on scenarios on questionnaires (Rodabaugh & Kravitz, 1994) investi-

TABLE 3

**Empirical Studies of Classroom Assessment
In College and University Classrooms**

Study	Context	Sample	Method	Findings
B. Brown, 1994	MBA program, repeating exam questions for a second section of a course versus using new items	9 students	Performance for same and different items on test	• Students did no better on items repeated from a previous section's exam than on new items.
Guthrie, 1992	Examining the goals, modes, and evaluation of instruction for faculty whose students demonstrated gains in analytical reasoning	239 faculty—92 from Stanford (research university), 106 from Ithaca (comprehensive college), 41 from Mills (women's liberal arts college)	Survey	• Evaluations emphasized the cognitive domain, put low weight on class participation. • Evaluations emphasized lower order cognitive skills, not the higher order skills for which their instruction was noted.
Hale, Shaw, Burns, & Okey, 1984	Science problem solving	150 students, 9th grade through college science and science education courses	Computer-simulated multiple-choice test	• Test valid and reliable for assessing scientific problem solving

gated four hypotheses by manipulating conditions in the scenarios. For example, they described a professor who did not return or discuss tests, did not discard ambiguous questions, and did not give partial credit for partially correct answers ("unfair condition") to randomly selected subjects, and described a professor who did these things ("fair condition") to other subjects. The four hypotheses were that (a) college students' judgments of instructors would be affected by the grades instructors assigned, (b) college students' judgments of instructors would be affected by the fairness of procedures instructors used, (c) the effect of procedural fairness would be stronger than the effect of grades, and (d) selection of instructors ("would you take a course from this instructor?") would

TABLE 3 (continued)

Study	Context	Sample	Method	Findings
Jacobsen, 1993	Liberal arts college instructors noted by students to be exceptionally good at test preparation	15 sections, 13 instructors, 27 randomly selected students	Studied 15 sections (90th percentile or above in "preparing examinations" course evaluation)—survey, interview, and administrative data	• On average, small classes, upper-division courses, higher grades, performance classes, full professor and instructor ranks overrepresented but variability was apparent • Students liked methodical approach to evaluation, skill development in one defined area, some student choice, opportunity to explain answers; *disliked* comparison with other students
Larson, 1995	Portfolio use in baccalaureate colleges II	395 institutions, academic vice presidents or deans	Survey	• 202 institutions reported using portfolios; 47% of them used portfolios for classroom assessment • Contents included papers, projects, journals, self-evaluations, faculty evaluations, videos, and drafts
O'Sullivan & Johnson, 1993	Using performance assessments in a graduate-level educational measurement course	29 students and 29 students in a comparison group	Questionnaire	• Students who participated in a class where grading was performance based increased their competency.

TABLE 3 (continued)

Study	Context	Sample	Method	Findings
Rodabaugh & Kravitz, 1994	Psychology and education classes	300 students, equal numbers majoring in psychology, education, and other; 74% female; 50% traditional age/50% older; 45% Hispanic, 37% white, 9% African American; first-year students through post-BA	Survey study, 3 experiments with differing scenarios, each with 5 dependent variables: perceived caring by professor, respect from professor, students' liking of professor, professor's fairness, students' choice of professor. First experiment studied effects of fairness of testing procedures and student outcomes; second experiment studied effects of fairness of classroom policies and policies' effects on grades; third experiment studied effects of professor's fairness and warmth, lecturing ability, and difficulty of course.	• Effects were found on students' perceptions of caring, respect, liking, and choice for both grades received (lower grade distributions were associated with lower ratings) and procedural fairness (fair procedures were associated with higher ratings). • Effects for procedural fairness were much stronger than the effects for grades or for other behaviors of the instructor (warmth, lecturing ability, course difficulty). • No difference by gender, ethnicity, major, or GPA, except that older students were more rejecting of the unfair professor.

be more strongly affected by perceptions of fairness than by perceptions of personal warmth, lecturing ability, or course difficulty (p. 71). For the first three hypotheses, the judgments investigated were (a) perceptions of the instructor's caring for students, (b) perceptions of students' respect for the instruc-

TABLE 3 (continued)

Study	Context	Sample	Method	Findings
Stearns, 1996	Research and statistics class	8 students in control class, 25 students in experimental class	Experiment involved individual exam, then group exams, with discussion; took average of both scores for course tests. Control: individual exam; Dependent variable: final exam scores to measure retention of material	• Group exam section had higher scores on the final • Individual exam needs to be given first and counted to motivate all to come prepared.

tor, (c) degree to which students reported liking the instructor, (d) perceptions of instructor's fairness, and (e) reported likelihood of taking another class from the instructor, all measured on 6-point scales from very negative to very positive.

Results were striking in their clarity: Procedural fairness affected students' perceptions of the instructor and his or her course. Some evidence suggested that this effect was stronger for older students. Implications for an instructor's behavior are obvious—most notably that fairness, especially in testing procedures, is very important to students (Rodabaugh & Kravitz, 1994). A professor who is perceived as fair in testing and fair in establishing classroom policies will be respected, liked, perceived as caring, and likely to be chosen for another class. Conversely, a professor who is not perceived as fair will not be as well respected, liked, or chosen even if he or she gives relatively high grades.

These findings are quite compatible with the instructional and assessment principles that stress learning goals for students should be set intentionally, then clearly communicated to students at the outset of the course to maximize their motivation and learning—and that students' learning is even more important than students' liking the professor. Students should know where they are aiming when they do their work in the course: reading, writing, and all their activities and assignments. Even when students are listening to lectures, the learn-

Results were striking in their clarity: Procedural fairness affected students' perceptions of the instructor and his or her course.

---

ing goals they perceive are their intended direction will shape what they hear, how they comprehend, and how they conceptualize and store the information. Assessment should gather information about students' achievement of those goals, measured against clear, fair, and clearly communicated standards of quality. Comparing students' work to a standard of quality—criterion referencing—is the most appropriate form of assessment in most classrooms. Rodabaugh and Kravitz's study demonstrated that students perceive criterion referencing as fair and appropriate.

ENSURING THE QUALITY OF CLASSROOM ASSESSMENT INFORMATION

The information conveyed by grades, scores, ratings, or judgments of student assessments must be just that—information. Scores and grades must carry real meaning and be accurate indicators of that meaning. Further, the meaning of grades and scores must be appropriate for the purposes to which users of their information will put them. This section briefly defines the measurement principles of validity and reliability, shows how they apply to classroom assessment in higher education, and then discusses ways to enhance the validity (meaningfulness and appropriateness) and reliability (accuracy) of assessment information about students. It also includes practical suggestions about how to maximize the validity and reliability of classroom assessments that have been culled from a variety of resources (Linn & Gronlund, 1995; Nitko, 1996; Northwest Regional, 1994, 1998; Stiggins, 1997). Suggestions were chosen for their applicability to higher education, and examples illustrate uses in higher education classrooms.

Validity

Validity refers to the degree to which a score is meaningful and appropriate for its intended purpose. Validity refers, then, to whether and to what degree a score means what the instructor thinks it means, or says it means. Validity is a characteristic of a score put to a particular use, not a characteristic of a test or assessment itself. Messick (1989) distinguishes between the purposes of interpreting and using scores. In higher education classrooms, almost all assessment information is used. Formative feedback to students intended to guide their studying and summative assessment intended to be part of a course grade are both uses in Messick's terms. The use to which assessment information is put determines what kind of information is needed.

For example, a very carefully constructed final exam for an intermediate French class might produce valid measures of students' achievement in that class, but the same exam would not be a valid measure of students' achievement in a chemistry class. Although this example is obvious and a little silly, the same principle applies to misinterpretations of measures that are a lot less obvious. That same carefully constructed final exam for the intermediate French class might be a less valid measure of achievement in a different French class where the instructor pursued somewhat different goals for learning.

Validity is arguably the most important quality of a score from a classroom assessment, because such scores are used for educational decisions with consequences for students: deciding what content needs to be reviewed, assigning grades, counseling students about what courses to take in the future, deciding how a course might be taught differently. It is therefore imperative that the scores actually mean what the instructor thinks they mean; otherwise, unwise or unfounded decisions might be made. Appropriate consequences, and lack of inappropriate consequences, are one source of important evidence about the meaning of scores (Messick, 1989).

Maximizing the validity of information obtained from classroom assessments means maximizing the degree to which the scores, grades, ratings, or judgments contribute to making meaningful decisions about students' achievement or performance of intended goals for learning. To that end, the instructor should check to see that the intended learning goals themselves are appropriate ones for the course, the discipline, and the students; that assessments match the goals; and that the assessments' content matches the particular intended use. Table 4 shows the general principles for checking these conditions.

Score information is likely to match learning goals if items or tasks for students are clear, the content material matches the content of learning goals for the course, and each portion of the material contributes the appropriate weight or proportion of the total score. The level of thinking required for the assessment should match goals for the course, as should the demonstration modality, the actual task the assessment poses for the student. A complete and representative sample of the content and skills to be measured ensures "content validity."

The first way to ensure this match is through careful planning—that is, thinking about assessment at the start of overall planning for the course and continuing through constructing the syllabus and designing individual class activities. What kind of information is needed? What performances by students will give that information? The second way to ensure a match is to write test items or performance assessment tasks carefully and thoughtfully, keeping this principle in mind. It helps to have someone else who is familiar with the course material review the assessment tasks. For classroom assessments in higher education, a careful content review is the most important tool for ensuring validity.

TABLE 4

Validity of Classroom Assessments

Score information is likely to match learning goals if:

- Items or tasks for students are clear.

- Content material matches content of learning goals.

- Each portion of the material contributes the appropriate weight or proportion of the total score.

- The level of thinking (recall, application, analysis, synthesis, evaluation) required for the assessment matches the learning goal.

- The demonstration modality matches the intended learning goal. (Was the intent to identify something, describe something, make something, or do something?)

- The range of possible items or tasks or contexts is wide enough to represent accurately the goal for learning.

- Items or tasks are substantively representative of the nature of intended learning tasks.

Score information is likely to match the intended use for the information if:

- For grading, items or tasks represent all the course's goals for learning.

- For instruction, information is fine grained enough to determine not just that students can or cannot give correct answers, but what their misconceptions are.

- For placement, scores represent all the relevant and necessary background knowledge and skills.

A "test blueprint" or table of specifications is a method that helps to plan the appropriate content representation when writing tests and examinations. It also makes actually writing the test, or selecting items from a pool of items that are already written, easier and faster. Table 5 provides an example of a test blueprint for an exam in a sports medicine class.

Write the content to be covered in rows and the level of thinking required in columns. Taxonomies of educational objectives or a discipline-specific set of performance modalities can be used for this purpose. The important point is to use a way of classifying that is appropriate to the course. For many purposes, especially for introductory or survey courses, a simple two-category designation that distinguishes recall of information from memory and application of infor-

TABLE 5

A Test Blueprint for a Cumulative Final Exam in Evaluating Injuries

Learning goal	Recall	Application	Total
• Identify signs and symptoms of common pathologies	30	15	45 (39%)
• Identify anatomical locations	15	20	35 (30%)
• Describe special tests and evaluations	15	10	25 (22%)
• Make preliminary diagnoses based on knowledge of anatomy, pathology, and evaluation	0	10	10 (9%)
Total	60 (52%)	55 (48%)	115 (100%)

Source: Adapted from Platt, Turocy, & McGlumphy, 1998.

mation or problem solving would be as useful as a more complicated classification system.

The second step is to indicate, in the cells created by the rows and columns, the number of points that should be allocated for that particular content and level of thinking. For objective test items, one point usually means one item. For essay and partial credit items, the number of items will vary. If, for example, 10 points should be allocated to a cell, it could be one 10-point test item, two 5-point items, one 4-point and one 6-point item, and so on. Cells should be left blank (or given a zero) if it is not necessary to test that content at that level. Thus, totals and percents of the whole for each row and column allow a quick check for the distribution of score meaning. It is easy to see whether some content or type of thinking has been given too much weight, or too little, and adjust the blueprint accordingly before the instructor has spent a lot of time writing test questions.

This scheme should not get too complicated. Too many cells with too few points per cell suggests a microengineering of scores that is more precise than most classroom assessments will bear. A test blueprint should not be time consuming. It should function as a way to sketch out the plans for a test before writing it, ensuring appropriate coverage and saving time in the long run. It is much easier for an instructor to write five good recall items about atomic structure or write 10 points worth of application questions about global warming than to start with a blank page and the task "write an exam."

A score is likely to represent the content or performance domain if enough items or tasks are included so that the instructor can be confident performance level is not just a fluke or chance event, if the range of possible items or tasks or contexts is wide enough, and if items or tasks are substantively representative of the nature of intended learning tasks. Test blueprints help plan content coverage. For example, suppose an exam were supposed to cover the eight assigned readings for a section of a course in 20th century American novels but included questions about only two of the novels. If that section of the course were assessed only with that exam, then the portion of the grade that test was worth would treat that score as if it assessed knowledge of all five novels, no matter what the instructor had meant by the exam. Would the instructor be sure the students understood and could discuss all five novels? How much would confidence rise about the representativeness of the exam score if three novels were included?

Simple content representativeness is one issue in using test items or performance tasks to represent learning goals. Another issue is the representative nature of the task. Do the tasks students are asked to perform represent the kind of tasks the instructor had in mind for learning goals in the course? If the instructor's intent is that students should be able to discuss the use of Shakespearean images and references in contemporary American literature, what is the most representative kind of task to ask students to do? A paper requiring them to look up references and cross-references and deal with them in depth comes much closer than an essay test question where all the references must be recalled, because "discussion" will be limited to the size of the student's short-term memory.

Sketching out a course-level blueprint is a good idea for grading to make sure that the "score" that is the grade for the course contains the right proportions of different indexes from different assignments, projects, or exams for each of the course's intended learning outcomes. Sometimes a simple list-style blueprint will suffice for planning proportional representation of components in course grades. In assigning course grades, it is much more likely that the grade will match its intended use—namely, to indicate the achievement level for the whole course—if assessments represent all the learning goals for the course.

To be useful for instructional decisions—for example, deciding which goals to spend more or less time on—scores must give detailed information. One overall score, for example, on a final exam or paper is enough to use for grading purposes, but if scores on a midcourse assessment are to be used to influence future instruction, the scores must be on individual aspects of the goals. Did the students have difficulty with finding the material, with comprehending it and reasoning about it once they found it, or with the writing of the paper? Each aspect has different implications for what to reteach or review. One overall score indicating all three would not give the instructor this information. Or, on a midterm exam, it might be helpful to give separate scores for separate groups of knowledge or skills so that students know their strengths and weaknesses and can study accordingly, and so the instructor can aim instruction to hit the weaknesses harder than the strengths.

Reliability
Reliability refers to the degree to which a score is consistent, across time or judges or forms of assessment. With regard to consistency across time, it should not matter whether a final exam is scheduled on a Wednesday morning or a Thursday afternoon of finals week; given the same level of study and preparation, students should expect to receive the same exam grade no matter which day they take the exam. With regard to consistency across judges, for example, when a particular essay is scored in four sections of a freshman composition course with the same learning goals, one instructor should not have "easier" or "harder" standards for marking than another. And with regard to consistency across forms, consider the case of a student who takes a makeup exam. If the exam is to give the same assessment information as the original test, say to cover the same set of learning objectives and count as the same percentage of the course grade, then it should allow the student to score approximately what he or she would have scored had the student taken the regular exam with the rest of the class.

For "mental measurements"—measurements of achievement or other inside-the-head constructs—accuracy and consistency are confounded in a way that they are not for physical measurements. If a bathroom scale always reads exactly 2 pounds light, it is consistent but not accurate. It is possible to know that the scale is 2 pounds light, however, only because external and independent measures exist of what a "pound" is, against which the scale can be evaluated. No such external measures exist for learning goals in classes. The only available information about those goals comes from the measuring tools, the exams and assignments and projects, used to measure achievement in the course. So consistency and accuracy are completely confounded; the best available information about a student's "true" level of performance comes from measurements of performance that, at whatever level, are at least stable for the student.

This confounding of consistency and accuracy places a special burden on classroom assessments. In a physics lab, it is possible to measure an object 10 times, take the average of the measurements, and use the result as a reliable estimate of the object's true measure. For standardized assessments, it is possible at least some of the time to recruit subjects who take the same assessment twice to examine how consistent performance is. But it is not possible to do so for classroom assessments. Once an assessment is given, it is "over," and even if an instructor could persuade a few students to take it again (an unlikely event), the students would know what the questions were and would prepare for them, making it not the same assessment. As common checks for consistency are not available for measures of achievement in the classroom, instructors must take particular care to consider reliability when they design, write, and score classroom assessments.

Reliability and validity are related. Simple consistency, for its own sake, is not particularly helpful. A measure can be consistent but be the wrong measure for the job, as in the case of the French exam given in chemistry class that would reliably indicate, over and over, that the students did not know much French. But a score cannot be any more valid than it is reliable. If assessment results cannot be counted on to do a pretty good job of estimating students' real levels of achievement, they cannot carry much meaning. A very unreliable score, of any learning goal, might just as well represent a chance drawing from a fishbowl as performance on an assessment. The more reliable the score, the more it makes sense to ask "reliable indicator of what?"—and the "what" leads back to validity, the main concern. Viewed in this manner, the value of ensuring reliability in classroom measures lies in its contribution to validity, to maximizing the potential of information to be truly representative of a student's performance and thus useful to instructors and their students. Table 6 presents principles for maximizing the reliability of classroom assessments.

TABLE 6

Reliability of Classroom Assessments

Score is likely to represent consistent, typical performance for students if:

- Performance does not depend on time of day, location, or other external factors.

- Performance is consistent with other of the student's similar work.

- Enough items or tasks are included so that the instructor can be confident performance is not just a fluke or chance event.

Score is likely to represent a typical judgment (for rubrics and partial credit) if:

- Different judges would agree on the score.

- The halo effect and other potential biases have been avoided.

- The performance, not the student, has been rated.

A score is likely to represent consistent, typical performance for students if performance does not depend on time of day, location, or other external factors, and if performance is consistent with other of the student's similar work. These requirements are not usually great problems for classroom assessment in higher education—except, perhaps, in the event a statistics exam is given in a room next to some construction featuring an air hammer on concrete. In that case, day, time, and location can make a difference!

Checking to see whether performance is consistent with other work the student has done and with expected levels of performance given what the instructor knows about the student can be done informally. The classic example is something instructors have been doing for years: comparing out-of-class work with in-class work. If out-of-class work is outstanding but in class a student does poorly, chances are the out-of-class work is not entirely the student's own. This kind of judgment must be made with a clear picture of the achievement targeted in mind. Written work done outside class, for example, might be expected to benefit from spell checkers and extra editing time. These benefits would not be evidence of unreliability but would rather demonstrate performance on a task that differs from an in-class essay.

It is important to base expectations for students' performance on similar work. Individuals sometimes differ specifically in their achievement levels on various types of tasks and in various subject matters. Therefore, some students' work on one kind of task, say writing, may not match their work on another kind of task, say recall. Or students' achievement of learning goals related to the American Revolutionary War may differ from their achievement of learning goals related to the Civil War. A Civil War hobbyist, for example, might do much better on a Civil War assessment, and a student who had already had a course in 18th century British history might do much better on the Revolutionary War assessment. The whole point of a college course is for students to learn, and it is likely that students who study will do just that. Therefore, performance that goes up after instruction, because of studying, does not indicate unreliability.

A source of unreliable classroom assessments that is more likely to pose a problem than inconsistency across time is inconsistent judgments. Rater or judge errors are difficult to check in classroom assessment, because typically one instructor does all the grading for one class or section. Instructors do not usually grade work for each other's students. In some places, to do so might even be considered a violation of academic freedom. But it remains an important issue that the quality of the work is judged according to some specified standard and does not depend on which instructor's section a student schedules (Mitchell, 1998). This issue is not relevant for objectively scored tests, but it is very important when partial credit points or scoring schemes are used for essay tests and performance assessments. For these scoring schemes, a score is likely to represent a typical judgment if different judges would agree on the score and if the judgment is not influenced by irrelevant characteristics of students such as gender, expressed interest, and previous work.

Most instructors realize they must judge the work, not the student. But it is sometimes hard to bracket and ignore other information about the student when reading or observing a student's work. One such bias is so common it has a name: the "halo effect"—the phenomenon at work when a good answer to one problem influences the grader to ascribe more merit to the answers to subsequent problems than they actually deserve. The usual advice to avoid this problem is to grade all answers to the same problem at once, thus making implicit comparisons from one answer to the next on the same paper impossible.

Grading all the answers to one problem together has another benefit for reliability as well. The instructor will get used to the criteria and scoring scheme for that problem and be more likely to apply them uniformly to everyone's work if the same problem is graded over and over. It is mentally a much more difficult chore for the grader to use one set of criteria for one problem and then change criteria to grade each subsequent question than it is to repeat the process over again for each student's test.

A final but very important method for maximizing reliability of the rater is to work on the clarity of descriptions in scoring schemes. If each criterion and each point level within it has a clear description, the rater's task of recognizing that quality of work when he or she sees it is simplified. Clearly defined categories mean less room to guess about which category a work sample fits. When scoring schemes are clear, raters are likely to make consistent judgments themselves, from paper to paper, and they would be likely to agree with other raters if more than one person judges the same work.

Summary

"Validity" and "reliability" are used to describe the meaningfulness, appropriateness, and accuracy of scores and grades for their intended purposes. These characteristics of quality are of vital importance because without them, decisions will be based on misinformation. And instructors who work to ensure the validity and reliability of their classroom assessment information will realize another benefit beyond sound information about students' achievements. Instructors who have confidence in their information about students' achievements speak more confidently with students about their work, offer more helpful suggestions for improvement, and feel better about the effects of their instruction and their control of an effective means for monitoring and adjusting that instruction.

OPTIONS FOR CLASSROOM ASSESSMENT

A Framework for Understanding Assessment Options

Student assessment should be multidimensional and the focus of ongoing communication with students about their achievement of objectives for the course. The methodology for classroom assessment can be thought of as a toolkit that faculty members use for accomplishing their purposes. Students' involvement in assessment, at all stages of the process from design through scoring, is also recommended as a strategy for teaching and learning and for enhancing motivation.

Several versions of a framework for understanding types of classroom assessment have been offered (see Stiggins, 1992, 1997, particularly 1992). Assessment methods can be grouped into three general categories: paper-and-pencil tests, performance assessments of processes or products, and oral communication. For each category, objective (right/wrong or present/absent) and subjective (judgment of degree of quality) scoring can be developed. Objective scoring is easier to do than subjective rating, but objectively scored questions are more difficult to write well than are subjectively scored questions and exercises. Depending on the author one consults, portfolios can be considered a fourth category of assessment or a different sort of beast that falls between the cracks: part assessment method and part collection and communication of assessment results.

Different assessments are necessary to cover the full range of achievement targeted: knowledge, thinking, processes, products, and dispositions. Table 7 describes and gives some examples of the various kinds of assessments that can be used to evaluate achievement of learning goals.

Paper-and-Pencil Tests

College instructors are generally familiar with both objectively and subjectively scored tests. Test development should be keyed to the learning objectives for the course. It should be obvious to the student that what has been stressed in the course and what is valued knowledge are the focus of the exercises the students are asked to do. If, for example, a course had stressed interpreting poetry but a large portion of the final examination includes identifying poets, dates, and titles of poems, then scores on the final would not reflect what the instructor intended the students to learn, nor would they reflect what students thought they were supposed to learn.

TABLE 7

Classroom Assessment Options

	Objective scoring	Subjective scoring	Most appropriate uses	Major advantages	Potential pitfalls
Paper-and-pencil tests	Multiple choice, true/false, matching, fill in the blanks	Essays or show-the-work problems judged with rubrics or rating scales	To assess knowledge and thinking over a range of content or to assess dispositions and interests (ungraded)	Most reliable way to assess knowledge and thinking in a content area domain; best way to cover a large number of facts and concepts	Require clearly written items that appropriately sample a range of content material; easiest to write recall-level questions
Performance assessments	Judgments of performance on a task using a checklist	Judgments of performance on a task using rubrics or rating scales	To assess in-depth thinking in one area or to assess skills attained or products created	Allow measurement of in-depth thinking, skills, or products not readily assessable by tests	Require clear expectations for tasks and scoring to provide meaningful assessment information
Oral questions	In-class questions with right/wrong answers	Discussions or interviews evaluated with rubrics or rating scales	To assess knowledge and thinking during instruction or to assess dispositions and interests (ungraded)	Provide feedback for instruction; identify students' concepts and misconceptions; tap students' interests and opinions	Students may prefer not to speak up or give their honest responses in class.
Portfolios	Could use a checklist for portfolio entries but not recommended except for special purposes	Collection of a student's work and reflections over time; entries can be rated separately or as a whole	To document progress or development or to showcase complex achievement of a range of skills	Allow for assessment of student's development and some ownership and control by student	Require clear purpose, focused construction, and long-term attention to give any more useful information than stand-alone assessments

Source: Adapted from Stiggins, 1987, 1992, 1997.

To design a test, the learning targets must first be identified and then assessed to decide whether they represent knowledge, thinking, skills, products, or dispositions. Knowledge and thinking are usually captured well by well-written tests, but if the target includes skills or products, a test will be only a proxy for complete assessment. Two steps are necessary to make sure the test really taps into students' knowledge or thinking and not something else. The first is to design the general form of the exam, giving space and weight to various topics as appropriate to the instructional intent. A test blueprint can help accomplish this aim. The second step is to write clear, unambiguous test questions. Students can help with this step, but instructors who ask students to write questions should make sure that final, edited items are well written, according to the guidelines in this subsection, and that the final set of items used for a test matches its blueprint.

Objective test items

Table 8 presents some general guidelines for writing objective test items. The purpose of these dos and don'ts is an important one that contributes to the validity of the information instructors will get from students' performance on the test. If a test item is written in such a way as to tap into general logic or cleverness, then a student's score will reflect general ability as well as the particular knowledge or application that the instructor meant to teach. General cleverness is not a bad quality, but it is not the basis on which a student's work in a course should be judged. A poorly written test item also increases the risk that students who know how to answer the question will get it wrong, which will cause the test score to reflect less achievement of whatever the course was designed to teach than is actually the case.

Each "do" and "don't" has a reason behind it. For example, the suggestion to put matching and multiple-choice answers in logical order, if there is one, is to save students who know the answer some reading and processing time they should be spending on the substance of the test material. If the question is "In what year was the Battle of Hastings fought?" some students may need to look over a list of choices and decide among them. But for some students, answering this question is really a matter of saying to themselves, "Where did she put 1066?" If the dates are listed in order, it is easier to answer such a question, and the student can answer the question

TABLE 8

Dos and Don'ts for Writing Objective Test Items

General

1. Use clear and concise language.
2. Prepare a draft and edit it.
3. Proofread the draft from a student's point of view.
4. Test important ideas, not trivial points.
5. Write short, clear directions for *all* sections of the test.
6. Don't copy statements from the textbook.

True/false items

1. Make statements definitely true or definitely false.

   NOT: The advent of the computer is the strongest force for social change in the 20th century.
   BETTER: Some authors have compared the social impact of the advent of the computer with that of the printing press.

2. Keep statements short.

3. Have only one idea per statement.

   NOT: Captain Ahab was not afraid of death, whereas Ishmael wanted very much to live.
   BETTER: Captain Ahab was not afraid of death.

4. Use positive statements; if the statement contains a "not," highlight it.

   NOT: The issue of the Emancipation Proclamation in 1863 did not result in immediate freedom for any slaves.
   BETTER: The issue of the Emancipation Proclamation in 1863 did NOT result in immediate freedom for any slaves.

5. Make "trues" and "falses" about the same length.

6. Avoid patterns of answers (e.g., TTFF or TFTF).

Writing good test items is a skill that requires practice, drafting, editing, and all the other elements of good writing in any format.

quickly and move on, saving his or her serious thinking for more important parts of the test. Alphabetical order works well for lists of names or places. If no logical order is apparent, or if putting the answers in order would give clues to the answers of other items on the test, then the choices should be scrambled for the same reason—to have students' scores be as accurate a representation as possible of what they really know.

Writing good test items is a skill that requires practice, drafting, editing, and all the other elements of good writing in any

Matching items

1. Number the items in the first column; letter the response choices in the second column.
2. Make items and response choices homogeneous.

NOT: Match the word with its definition.

1.	Solid bodies bounded by planar surfaces	a. Absolute zero
2.	At a constant temperature, the volume of a given amount of gas varies inversely with pressure.	b. Boyle's law
		c. Crystal
3.	Temperature at which the kinetic energy of molecules is zero	d. Enthalpy of
4.	Process of passing from solid to gas without going through the liquid state, or vice versa	fusion
		e. Ionic radii
5.	Heat required to melt 1 mole of a substance	f. Sublimation

BETTER: Match each gas law with the name of the scientist associated with it.

1.	The volume of a certain mass of gas is inversely proportional to the pressure, at constant temperature.	a. Avogadro
		b .Boyle
2.	The total pressure in a mixture of gases is the sum of the individual partial pressures.	c. Charles
		d. Dalton
3.	The rates of diffusion of two gases are inversely proportional to the square roots of their densities.	e. Graham
		f. Kelvin
4.	Equal numbers of molecules are contained in equal volumes of different gases if the temperature and pressure are the same.	
5.	The volume of a given mass of gas is directly proportional to the absolute temperature, at constant pressure.	

3. Each response choice should look like a plausible answer for any item in the set. If not, the list is not similar enough to be a set of matching items.
4. Keep the lists short (5 to 10 items).
5. Separate longer lists into two or more shorter ones, using the principle of homogeneity.
6. Avoid having the same number of items and response choices so that the last answer is not really a choice.
7. Put the longer phrases in the left column and the shorter phrases in the right column.
8. Arrange response choices in a logical order, if there is one.
9. Avoid using incomplete sentences as items.
10. Keep all items and response choices in a set on the same page of the test.

Completion/fill-in-the blank items

1. Don't put too many blanks together.

   NOT: The _____ left _____ over issues of _____.
   BETTER: The Puritans left England over issues of _____.

2. Make the answer a single word if possible.
3. Make sure there is only one way to interpret the blank.

   NOT: Abraham Lincoln was born in _____. (A log cabin? Poverty? Kentucky? 1809? A bed?)
   BETTER: Abraham Lincoln was born in the year _____.
   OR: In what year was Abraham Lincoln born? _____

4. A word bank (a set of choices in a box or list) is often helpful, depending on whether total recall is important or not and whether spelling counts.

TABLE 8 (continued)

Multiple-choice items

1. The stem (the numbered section) should ask or imply a question.
2. If the stem is an incomplete sentence, the alternatives should be at the end and should be the answer to an implied question.
3. If "not" is used, underline it.
4. Avoid statements of opinion.
5. Don't link two items together so that getting the second one correct depends on getting the first one correct.

   NOT: 1. What is the next number in the series 1, 5, 13, 29, . . . ?
   a. 43   b. 57   c. 61   d. 64
   2. What is the following number in the series in question #1?
   a. 122   b. 125   c. 127   d. 129

   BETTER: 1. What is the next number in the series 1, 5, 13, 29, . . . ?
   a. 43   b. 57   c. 61   d. 64
   2. What is the next number in the series 1, 4, 16, 64, . . . ?
   a. 128   b. 256   c. 372   d. 448

6. Don't give away the answer to one item with information or clues in another item.
7. Use three to five functional alternatives (response choices). Silly alternatives (e.g., "Mickey Mouse") do not draw serious consideration and should not be used. To inject humor into a test, use a whole silly item, not part of a serious one.
8. All alternatives should be plausible answers for those who are truly guessing.
9. Repeated words go in the stem, not the alternatives.

   NOT: Computer-based tutorials are called "adaptive" if they change based on information
   a. about the student.
   b. about the content material.
   c. about the computer.

   BETTER: Computer-based tutorials are called "adaptive" if they change based on information about the
   a. student.
   b. content material.
   c. computer.

10. Punctuate all alternatives correctly, given the stem.
11. Put the alternatives in logical order, if there is one.
12. Avoid overlapping alternatives.

    NOT: Which of the following possibilities enabling communication over the Internet is the best choice for a class discussion in a distance learning course?
    a. E-mail
    b. Usenet news
    c. Chat systems
    d. Conferencing software

    BETTER: Which of the following possibilities enabling communication over the Internet is the best choice for a class discussion in a distance learning course?
    a. E-mail
    b. Usenet news
    c. Chat systems

13. Avoid "all of the above" as an alternative.
14. Use "none of the above" sparingly.
15. Adjust the difficulty of an item by making the alternatives more or less alike. The more similar the alternatives, the more difficult the item.

Note: For more detail, see Linn & Gronlund, 1995; Nitko, 1996; Ory & Ryan, 1993.

format. Writing unambiguous test items is a more understandable task after an instructor has studied the reasons behind each suggestion. (See the resources described in "Conclusions and Further Resources for Faculty.")

Essays and partial-credit problems

Assessing thinking and problem solving is a good use of the time and effort it takes to read and score essay tests or show-the-work and partial-credit problems in math or science. To really assess thinking, and not merely recall, the question must present a new problem to the student, one that he or she has not seen before. The question does not have to be truly *new,* just new to the student. As described earlier, even the most complex reasoning question becomes a matter of recall if the textbook or class discussion has already laid out the reasoning for students.

This approach will sound harsh to instructors who are used to hearing complaints about exams: "We never went over that in class." The way around this complaint is to make sure that class time includes work on new problems, students' analysis of issues, and the like, so that students understand why new thinking is important and called for, and learn how to do it. The solution is *not* to preview everything on a test; otherwise, no higher order thinking can be demonstrated. Table 9 presents some suggestions for writing essay questions.

Only the instructor of the class can determine what is new and what is not. Consider the example of a freshman English class that is reading the Declaration of Independence. An essay question about the structure and persuasiveness of Jefferson's argument could require thorough, original thought—or not! Suppose a whole class period had been devoted to discussing "the structure and persuasiveness of Jefferson's argument." Then this question would tap students' recall of the day's discussion.

This point about novelty of problem and level of thought required from the student shows clearly that assessment and instruction are related enterprises. Many authors have polemicized that assessment and instruction *should* be related and have demonstrated ways to do it well. But whether an instructor realizes or intends it or not, assessment and instruction *will* be related, because both are experiences the student has with material he or she is supposed to learn. Therefore, it is important for instructors to understand the

TABLE 9

Dos and Don'ts for Writing Essay Test Items

Restricted range essay items (usually one to three paragraphs per answer)

1. For most purposes, use several restricted essays rather than one extended essay.
2. Ask for a focused response to one point; state the question so the student can tell what kind of response is required.
3. Do not ask a question that requires merely extended recall. Questions should require some critical thinking; for example:

   - explain causes and effects
   - identify assumptions
   - draw valid conclusions
   - present relevant arguments
   - state and defend a position
   - explain a procedure
   - describe limitations
   - apply a principle
   - compare and contrast ideas.

4. Use clear scoring criteria.
5. Don't use optional questions.

Extended range essay items (answer will be a true "essay" form)

1. Use to test in-depth understanding of a small range of content.
2. Call for students to express ideas in an organized fashion. Specify both what should be discussed and how it should be discussed.
3. Allow enough time for students to think and write.
4. Assign the essay as a paper or theme if out-of-class time is needed or if students' choice and resources are required.

Note: For more detail, see Linn & Gronlund, 1995; Nitko, 1996.

nature of this relationship. Writing better essay questions and problems will be only one of many good results from this understanding. Consider the following scenario:

> *This is a true story. A colleague of ours teaches an introductory calculus section. Early one term, he and his class were working through some standard motion problems: "A boy drops a water balloon from a win-*

*dow. If it takes 0.8 seconds to strike his erstwhile friend,
who is 5 feet tall, how high is the window?" On the
exam, the problem took this form: "Someone walking
along the edge of a pit accidentally kicks into it a small
stone, which falls to the bottom in 2.3 seconds. How
deep is the pit?" One student was visibly upset. The question was not fair, she protested. The instructor had
promised that there would not be any material on the
exam that they had not gone over in class. "But we did
a dozen of those problems in class," our colleague said.
"Oh no," shot back the student, "we never did a single
pit problem."* (McClymer & Knoles, 1992, p. 33)

This illustration is used to introduce a discussion about how
"inauthentic" assessment leads students to develop problem-
solving strategies that help them pass exams but do not help
them reach the intended learning goals. The discussion goes
on to describe two categories of these maladaptive student
responses, "shapes" and "clumps," which are discussed later.

The student who had trouble with the "pit problem" had not
availed herself of a problem-solving strategy that the instructor
had recommended, namely, drawing the problem (McClymer
& Knoles, 1992, p. 34). Thus, her inability to solve this problem, and the low score that would result, would be an accurate
and meaningful (reliable and valid) reflection of her learning
about motion problems. The "inauthenticity" or contrived nature of the problem was not the only reason for her failure.

Viewed from the perspective of developing concepts, the
"pit problem" shows how true concept development and application skills require variation in instruction, not just in
novel problems on exams, and how the two are related.
When students learn concepts, they are learning a set of defining characteristics. The characteristics that are important
in a concept's definition are called "essential attributes."
Characteristics that just happen to be there, but are not relevant to the concept's definition, are called "nonessential attributes." The best way to teach a concept to learners who
are not familiar with it is to present the best examples, plus
some counterexamples, and include variation on all attributes that might plausibly be confused with the definition.

For example, an essential characteristic of a simile is that a
comparison of two like things is explicitly stated, commonly
with "like" or "as," and an essential characteristic of a meta-

phor is that the comparison is implied. Metaphor and simile are often taught together, so that the similarity (both are comparisons of two things that are alike in some way) and difference (one comparison is explicit, the other implicit) are easy to point out. This approach helps with development of the concept. A variety of examples are needed, too, so that students can learn which attributes are essential. All the examples should not be about flowers, or even always about concrete things, lest students get the mistaken idea or misconception that metaphors and similes have to compare things to concrete objects. Similarly, all the examples should not be from poems, lest students get the misconception that comparisons have to be in poetry to be called metaphors and similes.

During instruction, then, the series of motion problems should not all have been dropping-from-window problems. The collection of "dropping problems" could have included various settings, buildings, cliffs, holes, scaffolds, and so on, and the students could have been asked what they all had in common, forcing students to articulate what their working understanding of the concept was in time for further explanation if misconceptions were apparent. Then students' task would have been to recognize the novel "pit problem" on the test as one of the "dropping problems" they had learned how to solve. One suspects, however, from the authors' account and the instructor's suggestion that students draw the problems, that attention had already been paid to essential and nonessential attributes in that particular calculus class. The student who protested may have been demonstrating that she did not, in fact, understand the concept. If that is the case, then a low score on that problem would correctly indicate her lack of understanding.

When instructors do not attend well to concept development and make sure that examples and counterexamples are clear for students, students will sometimes, understandably, attune to aspects of the format of problems or arguments. After all, in their essays or solutions, students will be trying to convince the instructor who is grading their work that they deserve high scores. A well-constructed test will not compensate for a lack of concept development in instruction. If instruction has been appropriate, however, a well-constructed test and a carefully prepared scoring scheme can minimize cases when students score well because they were skilled at *appearing* to understand.

Two different ways that students present responses demonstrate a less than deep and critical understanding of concepts, problems, or arguments—"clumps" and "shapes" (McClymer & Knoles, 1992, pp. 38-39). Clumps are parts of arguments, solutions to problems, or critical analyses that pile up analytical elements without the logic and explanations that should hold them together. Three kinds of clumps include "data packing," in which students write many facts but do not make clear what the facts are intended to show; "jargon packing," in which students use much terminology to make it sound as though they understand but do not, in fact, explain anything with the terms; and "assertion packing," in which students report *that* something is the case (for example, that the poet John Donne used imagery) without identifying, explaining, or citing any actual evidence. Sometimes several of these clumps are used in the same essay or analysis.

Shapes are approximations of the logic of criticism, the form without the substance (or the words without the music). Students might copy the form of someone else's analysis, perhaps from a textbook, or uncritically apply an algorithm that looks as though it should fit without understanding why it is appropriate. Students may stick to a surface recitation of a piece of literature or textbook, demonstrating that they have read the material but not that they have used it to think critically. A third shape students sometimes use is a one-note analysis, describing part but not all of the meaning required to answer the question fully.

McClymer and Knoles (1992) interpreted students' tendencies to answer higher level questions with clumps and shapes in light of some survey data collected at their institution. Entering freshmen reported that their main responsibilities as students were to master informational content and acquire critical skills. They did not express much support for the purposes of becoming scholars in their own right. Freshmen are known to have this expert-oriented, content-based understanding of learning; eventually more personal ownership of knowledge and thinking abilities becomes important for those who make progress through the stages of adult intellectual development (Perry, 1970). There is some truth to the claim, however, that students in higher education will be interested in passing courses as well as in learning, as students have invested time and money in enrolling in courses. Good instruction, coupled with high quality assessment, can help them do both. Clear scoring plans can help instructors judge the quality of the range of students' responses, from incorrect, to clumps, shapes, and other approximations, to appropriate, clear, well-reasoned answers.

Scoring essays and partial-credit problems may be done by a point method or a rubric method. If the problem or essay is one that requires a discrete amount of information and one solution or organizational strategy, it is easy to set up a system assigning points for each aspect, with a total number of points for a complete, correct answer. The instructor must make sure that the points reflect the relative importance of each aspect's contribution to the whole. Some aspects that are more important than others may be worth more points. Moreover, total points for the essay must reflect that essay question's contribution to the whole test. If it does not, the question should be weighted accordingly. For example, if an essay should be worth 20 points on a test but it has only 10 logical points, the score for the essay should be doubled and then added to the rest of the score for the test.

Rubrics are descriptive rating scales that are particularly useful for scoring when judgment about the quality of an answer is required—when, for example, it is not so much that the student remembered all the right concepts and organized them correctly, but more that the essay was well conceived, strongly argued, included original perspectives, or the like. Rubrics are good at indicating a range of poor quality through excellent quality work, making them ideal for scoring many college-level essay questions, show-the-work problems, and performance assessments.

To write rubrics, begin with a description of the criteria for good work. Envision a well-constructed, complete, and clear answer to the question or problem. What would its important characteristics be? They should be directly related to the knowledge, critical thinking, or skills that the instructor intended the students to acquire, and therefore they ought to be related to activities and instruction for the course, what students read and studied, and therefore what students will expect the test to require.

List the criteria for good work, then describe levels of performance. Be careful to use descriptions (e.g., "grammar and usage errors are rare and do not interfere with meaning") rather than judgments (e.g., "good"). Use as many levels as there are meaningful distinctions. Meaning is more important than having some particular number of levels. The term "analytic rubrics" is used when each criterion has a separate scale and the essay is rated on each separately, with the several ratings summed or averaged for a total score. Table 10 presents an example of analytic rubrics. The term "holistic rubrics" is used when all criteria are considered together on one descriptive rating scale and the answer is scored at the level that best describes it. Table 11 presents an example of holistic rubrics using the same criteria. Rubrics can be shared with students ahead of time so they better understand what they are being asked to do and what counts as good work.

Two good ways to share rubrics also enable students' involvement in assessment, which in turn enhances motivation and learning. When instructors share the rubrics, they can also give students some examples of work done at various

TABLE 10
Analytic Rubrics for a Question on an Essay Test

Thesis and organization

4—Thesis is defensible and stated explicitly; appropriate facts and concepts are used in a logical manner to support the argument.

3—Thesis is defensible and stated explicitly; appropriate facts and concepts are used in a logical manner to support the argument, although support may be thin in places and/or logic may not be made clear.

2—Thesis is not clearly stated; some attempt at support is made.

1—No thesis or indefensible thesis; support is missing or illogical.

Content knowledge

4—All relevant facts and concepts included; all accurate.

3—All or most relevant facts and concepts included; inaccuracies are minor.

2—Some relevant facts and concepts included; some inaccuracies.

1—No facts or concepts included, or irrelevant facts and concepts included.

Writing style and mechanics

4—Writing is clear and smooth. Word choice and style are appropriate for the topic. No errors in grammar or usage.

3—Writing is generally clear. Word choice and style are appropriate for the topic. Few errors in grammar or usage, and they do not interfere with meaning.

2—Writing is not clear. Style is poor. Some errors in grammar and usage interfere with meaning.

1—Writing is not clear. Style is poor. Many errors in grammar and usage.

TABLE 11

Holistic Rubrics for a Question on an Essay Test

4—Thesis is defensible and stated explicitly; appropriate facts and concepts are used in a logical manner to support the argument. All relevant facts and concepts included; all accurate. Writing is clear and smooth. Word choice and style are appropriate for the topic. No errors in grammar or usage.

3—Thesis is defensible and stated explicitly; appropriate facts and concepts are used in a logical manner to support the argument, although support may be thin in places and/or logic may not be made clear. All or most relevant facts and concepts included; inaccuracies are minor. Writing is generally clear. Word choice and style are appropriate for the topic. Few errors in grammar or usage, and they do not interfere with meaning.

2—Thesis is not clearly stated; some attempt at support is made. All or most relevant facts and concepts included; inaccuracies are minor. Writing is not clear. Style is poor. Some errors in grammar and usage interfere with meaning.

1—No thesis or indefensible thesis; support is missing or illogical. No facts or concepts included or irrelevant facts and concepts included. Writing is not clear. Style is poor. Many errors in grammar and usage.

levels. Ask students to rate the examples and tell why they scored them as they did. If descriptions of levels are well written, students will have to articulate the qualities of the work to justify their ratings. A variation on this strategy is to share the examples of work with students and have the students reason inductively from the examples to write the rubrics themselves. This approach works well and helps students develop a sense of ownership of the criteria for good work. Students are also likely to internalize and remember these criteria for good work if they develop them themselves. The cost for this instructional benefit is time; therefore, it is wiser to use this strategy on very important and authentic work than on simpler, more contrived classroom assignments.

Performance Assessment

Performance assessment refers to assessment in which a student's product or participation in a process is observed and judged. Performance assessments have two parts: a task and a scoring scheme. One without the other constitutes an incomplete performance assessment.

Performance tasks differ from essay tests in that they usually require sustained performance, often allow the use of resources, and often encourage revision and refinement before a final product is submitted. (Suggested frameworks for categorizing assessments range from multiple choice at one end of the continuum to presentations [Bennett, 1993] or collections of work over time [Snow, 1993] at the other.) A performance task in which a student is asked to solve a problem and explain the solution in one or two class periods is closer in kind to an essay question than a performance in which a student is asked to write a paper about a research question, using library and Internet resources, over the course of a semester.

One benefit of some performance assessment tasks is the requirement that students write reflections or explanations. Writing explanations makes students' reasoning explicit. It is a no-lose situation: Either a student gives evidence of clear, logical, appropriate reasoning in a discipline or demonstrates where his or her reasoning is flawed, thus identifying specifically what area needs more work. Writing reflections affords students the opportunity to think about what they have learned and what it means. "Knowing what they know" is a metacognitive achievement for students, an awareness of comprehension that is required for students to become self-sustaining, self-directed learners in a discipline.

Performance assessment tasks should not be simply interesting, novel, or appealing activities chosen for their novelty or appeal. Performance tasks should be constructed to elicit evidence of learning outcomes achieved—which requires thought and care. The following example shows how thought must be given to performance tasks to ensure that they give evidence of students' achievement of specific learning targets. In the example, a novice teacher thinks it would be a good idea to make an assessment out of the instructional activity of putting the Socrates of Plato's *Apology* on trial (Wiggins, 1998). But what is wrong with that idea, and what should be done about it?

- *Although the desired achievement involves the text and its implications, the activity can be done engagingly and effectively by each student with only limited insight into the entire text and its context. If a student merely has to play an aggrieved aristocrat or playwright, he or she can study for that role with only a limited grasp of the text. Also, the student's trial performance need not have much to do with Greek life and philosophy. The question of assessment validity (Does it measure what we want it to measure?) works differently, requiring us to consider whether success or failure at the proposed task depends on the targeted knowledge (as opposed to fortunate personal talents): [The] performance of the student playing, say, one of the lawyers may be better or worse relative to his or her debating and lawyering skills rather than relative to his or her knowledge of the text.*

- *It is highly unlikely that we will derive apt and sufficient evidence of understanding of the text from each individual student through this activity, even if we can hear an understanding of the text in some comments by some students. In fact, in the heat of a debate or mock trial, students might forget or not be able to use what they understand about the text, depriving themselves and us of needed assessment evidence. This is a crucial problem, common to many proposed assessment tasks: [When] we employ a particular performance genre, such as a trial, essay, or report, as a means to some other assessment end, we may fail to consider that the performance genre itself is a variable in the task and will affect the results.*

- *Although the trial may provide some evidence, it is far more likely that in this case a thorough and thoughtful piece of writing, combined with an extensive Socratic seminar on the text, would tell us more of what we need to know about students' knowledge and understanding. Such writing and discussion can certainly supplement the trial, but in considering such an idea we should be alert to the fact that no single complex performance task is sufficient for sound assessment.* (pp. 31-32)

> **"Authentic assessment" means that assessment tasks, whether test questions or performance assessment tasks, are grounded in the kind of work people actually do in a discipline.**

Assessment should be both "authentic" and "educative" (Wiggins, 1998). "Authentic assessment" means that assessment tasks, whether test questions or performance assessment tasks, are grounded in the kind of work people actually do in a discipline. That is, tests are not inappropriate, but they should be used the same way that drills in athletic practice are, for mastery and review of component skills, while keeping in mind the end or goal of real work or performance in the discipline (Wiggins, 1998). And at least some of the time, the "game must be played," or real-world performance must be attempted, to help students see what is required for real practice and how they measure up. "Educative assessment" means that a primary purpose of students' participation in assessment is to teach, to help students improve on dimensions of performance that are required for genuine or authentic work, to help them conceptualize what that work looks like (Wiggins, 1998).

Scoring criteria for evaluating performance tasks are constructed in a similar manner to the scoring schemes used for essay test questions. Their content should reflect the nature of the process or product that is to be scored.

Criteria for evaluation can be used holistically, considering all criteria simultaneously and assigning a single score, or analytically, considering each criterion separately and assigning a separate score for each. Analytical scoring is more helpful as feedback to students than holistic scoring, because students can see where their strengths and weaknesses are and work on their skills accordingly. Holistic scoring takes less time, because one judgment is required of the scorer instead of many. Analytic and holistic rubrics for performance assessments are similar in form to rubrics for essays and partial-credit test problems.

Table 12 presents a set of rubrics for scoring a Web page design project, a performance assessment. It is an analytic rubric, chosen as an example here because two of its scales, HTML Creation Skills and Navigation, illustrate rather concrete descriptions of work at each level (e.g., "at least two lists"), while the Web Page Layout scale illustrates more abstract quality descriptions (e.g., "hierarchy closely follows meaning") that require substantive judgment. Both kinds of descriptions are appropriate for rubrics; the important point is that the descriptions match what genuinely reflects levels of quality. Depending on the purpose of the assignment, this set of rubrics could include a fourth scale to evaluate the accuracy, importance, or impact of the content included on the student's Web page.

Another way scoring scales can vary is with regard to whether they are generalized or task specific. Generalized rubrics can be used in assessment, but they also can be used instructionally, shared with students to help them understand the nature of the achievement target. Generalized rubrics are one way to communicate the characteristics of good quality work. Students can use them in their work and in evaluation of others' work. Task-specific scoring rubrics are easier to

TABLE 12

Performance Assessment Rubrics for a Web Page Design

Level 1	Level 2	Level 3	Level 4	Level 5
		Web page (HTML) creation skills		
No HTML formatting tags; text is not broken into paragraphs.	Text is broken into paragraphs; headings are used; no other HTML tags.	Headings, title, tags such as preformatted text, styles, centering, horizontal lines, lists, etc.	Same as Level 3 plus images and hyperlinks to related material.	Same as Level 4 plus at least 2 lists, images as hyperlinks; color or background image, frames, tables, or imagemap.
		Web page layout		
Layout has no structure or organization.	Text broken into paragraphs and sections.	Headings label sections and create hierarchy; some consistency.	Hierarchy closely follows meaning; headings and styles consistent within pages; text, images, and links flow together.	Consistent format; extends the information from page to page; easy to read; attention to different browsers and their quirks.
		Navigation		
One page	One page with title bar added, heading, etc.	Two pages (or one page with links within page or to other resources); navigation between pages; links work.	Three or more pages with clear order, labeling, and navigation between pages; all links work.	Title page with other pages branching off and at least four pages total; navigation path clear and logical; all links work.

Source: San Diego County, 1998. Used with permission.

apply reliably the first time, but they cannot be shared with students ahead of time, when the assignment is made, because they contain answers (e.g., "uses Newton's Law of Cooling" instead of "selects relevant principles and procedures").

Instructors who regularly involve students in their own assessment can use this distinction to advantage. Share generalized rubrics with students or have them develop their own rubrics, then present a specific task for students to work and then score together. In describing why a performance deserves a certain score, students will articulate the specifics. In the example above, students would defend a score by saying, "They selected Newton's Law of Cooling, which in this case was a relevant principle for solving the problem."

Grading cooperative assignments presents an unusual challenge. Performance assessment highlights this difficulty, because most cooperative assignments are some type of performance assessment. Group reports, skits, or other projects can result in performance by a group in cases where an individual paper or other assessment is not really feasible. Yet college grades are given to individuals. Table 13 presents an example of a peer evaluation that group members can use. If students are aware ahead of time of the expectations and the fact that they will be monitored, many problems will take care of themselves. If the peer evaluations indicate that one group member was not contributing at the same level as others, and if the instructor's observations agree, then the instructor can intervene in several different ways, from speaking to the student or group to adjusting the grade.

Oral Questions

Oral questions during class time help both instructors and students to clarify what they know and where misconceptions have occurred. They work best in small classes. The instructor must know students' names to call on them, and students must know their classmates well enough so that they do not perceive the questions as public grilling. Oral questions can be factual in nature and check for simple recall or for whether or not assigned reading was done. "Why did your author say that Thomas Jefferson became interested in education?" "What is the chemical reaction that happens during nuclear fission?"

For oral questions to indicate accurately what the class as a whole understands, it is important to sample a range of students. The range should include various abilities as well as various interests. Always calling on students who have their hands raised will bias the information gained about class mem-

TABLE 13

Sample Peer Evaluation for Cooperative Learning Assignments

Group members	Worked cooperatively to complete assignments	Attended and participated in scheduled meetings	Supported and respected other members' efforts and opinions	Prepared adequately for sessions	Made substantial contributions to group's under-standings—shared ideas, re-sources, information

Write the names of each member of the group, including yourself, in the boxes in the first column. Put a check in each cell in the grid to indicate "fine job, as expected" for each group member for each criterion. For any box in which you have reservations about making a check because a group member did not meet your expectations for a criterion, write a brief comment. For any box in which you would like to comment on truly exceptional performance, please do so.

Source: Adapted from Munson, 1995.

bers' understanding. Most of the time, a disproportionate number of students who do understand the material in a lesson will be represented among those who volunteer to participate.

Handled well, oral questions provide good assessment information for instructors about students' understanding and interest. This information is best interpreted for the group (class). The use of assessment information about individual's participation in class discussions for grading is more problematic, as personal and group dynamics as well as availability of "air time" mean such information gives an incomplete picture of an individual's understandings.

Ask students questions that require knowledge at all cognitive levels. As for test questions, it is easier to pose recall questions in class than to ask questions that require application of principles, analysis of issues, or other complex thinking. Similarly, it is easier to judge the adequacy of responses to recall questions than to questions requiring more thought. The kind of questions the instructor asks should match the kind of information the instructor needs to know. Preparing some higher order questions ahead of time is a good strategy, as questions made up on the spot in a class are likely to be recall questions. Asking "why" as a follow-up to concept questions is also a good way to elicit thinking from students.

Portfolios

A portfolio is a purposeful collection of a student's work, often with samples of work collected over time and with reflections about what was learned or what a piece is supposed to demonstrate (Arter, Spandel, & Culham, 1995; Nitko, 1996). Some authors consider portfolios an option for assessing work in their own right. Others consider portfolios a collection of various assessments. Portfolios constructed for a single course are usually designed to reflect achievement of the particular goals for that course. This purpose contrasts with the traditional artist's portfolio, which is designed to show best work in a field and may represent work done in several courses and outside courses. Some students, most notably in the fine arts, will develop such portfolios during their college careers, but they are not the focus of this discussion. The following review is limited to portfolios used to demonstrate achievement of learning goals for a course.

The most important point to decide when a portfolio is selected as an assessment tool is its purpose. What learning or accomplishments is it intended to show? And is it intended to illustrate progress, the process on the journey toward achievement, or just final products? A portfolio for a writing class, for instance, may include a series of drafts of various works with reflections on how revisions were made and what improvement was shown to demonstrate how a student understands the writing process, or it may be a collection of finished works to demonstrate the quality of final products.

Another consideration for portfolios is the extent to which a portfolio itself, as a collection, would be more valuable than the uncollected assessments individually. What would be gained by holding a collection of work over time, in one location and with periodic review, over simply assigning, discussing, and evaluating each assignment separately? For some purposes, such as demonstrating students' development into "writers" by showing how they have progressed, and for leaving the evidence where they will look over it repeatedly to reflect upon it (which in itself will contribute to develop-ment as a writer), the collection of work is the answer. But portfolios consume time and space, and if they are simply a storage box for a series of reports, they are not worth the extra time and space they take to construct and review.

For portfolios to be effective methods of assessment, it is essential to define clear and complete performance criteria against which the work will be compared (Arter, Spandel, & Culham, 1995). Although the criteria are used to score or grade students, it is not their most important function in a portfolio. The importance of criteria is to ensure that students use them as guides for selecting what goes into their portfo-lios and as guides for reflecting on their work. Thus, how the criteria are written is very important, because the language used in the criteria becomes the language in which descrip-tions of quality work are phrased. The contribution a portfo-lio can make that other forms of assessment commonly do not is this aspect of reflection by students, of living with and revisiting past work, of setting goals for future work and then evaluating whether and to what degree the goals were met.

A survey of academic vice presidents and deans at all Carnegie classification Baccalaureate College II institutions found that of 395 respondents, 202 used portfolios for insti-tutional outcomes assessment, classroom assessment, and/or other purposes such as admissions or placement (Larson, 1995). Those 202 administrators were sent a second survey, asking for more details, to which 101 responded. Among respondents using portfolios, 47% used them for classroom assessment. Administrators reported up to 29 years of class-room use of portfolios, with a mean of 6.4 years. The most common portfolio contents reported included final drafts of papers (50%), student projects (47%), journals/logs (41%), self-evaluations (35%), faculty evaluations (26%), videos (26%), and drafts of final work (23%). Selecting contents of portfolios used in the classroom included selection by faculty and student together (37%), selection by student using faculty guidelines (34%), selection by faculty alone (9%), and selection by student alone (4%). Rubrics or scoring schemes for evaluating classroom portfolios were reported as not used (44%), developed by faculty for institutional outcomes assessment (31%), developed by faculty to serve their own purposes (29%), developed by an accrediting agency (4%), and "other" (5%). Classroom portfolios were typically returned to the student (Larson, 1995).

On the positive side, administrators reported that portfolios were useful, powerful assessment tools whose chief strengths involved participation by students, the collection of multiple assessments, and the ability to demonstrate progress over time. On the negative side, administrators reported concerns about the logistics, accuracy, and grading of portfolios.

Summary
Options for classroom assessment include paper and pencil tests, performance assessment, oral questions, and portfolios. Each has its strengths and weaknesses and is particularly appropriate for different learning goals. Students' involvement in any of these methods increases their motivation, learning, and sense of ownership of the material. Once an instructor has decided what methods are most appropriate for assessing learning goals for students, it is important to communicate the decision to students. The syllabus is an appropriate place to do so. If a syllabus makes clear to students what their goals for learning are, how they will be assessed, and how those assessments will be combined for their course grade, students can monitor their own learning, itself a worthwhile goal for higher education.

ASSESSMENT IN THE DISCIPLINES

General principles for good assessment apply in all classes, no matter the discipline or course level. But the subject does matter. Achievement goals differ among disciplines and among course levels within disciplines. To decide what assessment is appropriate for a particular purpose in a particular class, an instructor needs to keep in mind the discipline-specific knowledge or skills to be assessed as well as the assessment principles that have been the focus of the first four sections.

If assessment of knowledge of a range of facts and concepts is required, as for an introductory survey course in a social or natural science, a paper-and-pencil test with objectively scored items is suitable. The important issue here is to make sure the questions are clearly written and that they represent a good sample of the content domain. If assessment of application of knowledge to original work of some sort is required, as for science laboratory skills, social science analysis of sources, or English use of literary devices in writing, then some sort of performance assessment is more appropriate than a test. The important issues are to make sure the task actually requires the knowledge and skills that the instructor intends to assess and to make sure that the scoring criteria accurately describe quality work.

Because the different disciplines do different work, instructors historically have focused on different aspects of assessment. For example, English instructors have long been concerned with the assessment of writing. A good source of ideas in the disciplines may be found through the various professional organizations, most of which have both publications and Web sites. Several resources are discussed in this section as examples, but they are by no means meant to be exhaustive. Readers are urged to look at the material from their own professional organizations through the lens of the assessment principles of validity and reliability.

Additional excellent examples from college courses in specific disciplines of student assessments and of sets of student assessments that make up whole courses and their grades may be found in *Effective Grading* (Walvoord & Anderson, 1998). These examples demonstrate good principles of assessment in the various disciplines and include assignments, scoring guides, and rationales for what the various instructors were trying to accomplish, in enough detail to serve as models that readers could use in their own courses. The book includes examples from biology, business management, composition, dental hygiene, economics, education, engineering, English, food and nutrition, history, mathematics, psychology, sociology, Spanish, statistics, and Western civilization.

Assessment plans should be part of planning for a course from the very beginning (Walvoord & Anderson, 1998), but often they are not. One way to approach this problem is for instructors to search in their professional literature for examples of activities or assignments that are meant to be instructional activities, and then see whether they can be adapted for assessment. Sometimes doing so will mean incorporating feedback and scoring mechanisms into the instructional activity and using the same activity for both purposes. It has the good effect of forcing the instructor to describe for the students the characteristics of good work, a step often overlooked in planning a course. Sometimes, a second version of the activity can be used for assessment after the first has been used as an instructional or practice activity. Another source of ideas for performance-based assessments is the work that professionals in the various disciplines actually do. Using these performances as the basis of classroom assignments and assessments is likely both to assess students' use of important knowledge and skills and to help students understand why they are learning the knowledge and skills in the first place. Too often classroom activities feel contrived and are not similar to real work, affecting their value for both assessment and motivation of students.

English/Language Arts

The assessment of writing is of major importance for college English classes. The language arts involve two types of writing: composition and literary analysis. Composition courses generally teach students how to write in various genres of literature. Literature courses teach students how to approach and analyze authors' premises, values, purposes, sense of audience, development of characters, use of imagery, and so on. Because the goals of instruction differ, appropriate assessment methods will emphasize different points. For composition courses, methods that involve students in the production and revision of writing are needed, with all that it implies. Students (or any authors) must be invested in a topic and have something to say about it before they can write well about it. Analytical skills are important for composition, but they rank behind expressive skills. For literature courses, analytical skills move to the forefront. Logical expression through structuring and supporting a good argument is possible only if students can develop defensible theses and gather supporting arguments and details. These differences show in performance assessments in both the tasks students are assigned and the scoring schemes or rubrics with which they are evaluated. Because the criteria for evaluation differ, feedback on students' work will also differ.

A body of research is available on providing feedback in composition classes. An investigation of the effects of a training seminar for new English teaching assistants on their grading of and feedback on student papers (Liggett, 1986) offers some thoughtful comments about grading papers. The author had 12 teaching assistants grade the same paper both before and after training, which included readings about assessment, seminar discussions, and practice with over 200 papers. "Before" and "after" papers were coded for format, placement, focus, and purpose of comments. The new teachers made more comments after training, more substantive comments instead of emotional comments such as "good!", and more comments about what the student was trying to say instead of the mechanics of expression. After training, new teachers were more confident that their feedback was appropriate and that their grades were, in fact, more reliable, demonstrating a higher level of agreement among graders, even though overall the grades for the same paper dropped slightly (Liggett, 1986).

After training and practice grading papers, and thus presumably after giving some thought to the process of grading papers and providing feedback, the new teachers changed roles. Before the seminar, their grading and feedback demonstrated their primary approach to their role was as editors; after the seminar, their primary approach was as instructors. The evaluation and judgmental aspects of the task, that is, actually assigning a grade, became more accurate (Liggett, 1986).

Moreover, some of the new teachers would have benefited from instruction in writing themselves. Their feedback indicated they were not always able to give good and appropriate responses to students' work, according with the general principle of assessment that instructors must have a good, clear grasp of the achievement target themselves to be able to teach the subject and assess students' knowledge of it (Liggett, 1986).

Liggett also surveyed high, medium, and low achievers of the 12 teaching assistants to describe their reaction to the feedback. Reaction was mixed. Students do not learn much when writing teachers "fix" their work by closely editing it for them, and many students recognized that point. Others preferred more specific feedback. Which kind of feedback is "best" depends on the purpose of the grading, a point that needs to be clarified for teachers of college English (Liggett, 1986). If the purpose is instruction, then substantive comments that help students think on their own are most helpful. If the purpose is judgment, then comments that help students see where they lost specific points are helpful. Conflicting purposes of evaluation continue to exist. Where conflicts exist, the function of instruction and education for students should take precedence (Walvoord & Anderson, 1998; Wiggins, 1998). In this case, it means that instructors' "editing" students' work is less desirable than instructors' comments that point students in a direction to edit their own work.

Written feedback is an important but complex area of study in its own right. Teachers' comments on essays can foreclose students' thoughts too soon, turning revisions into "what the teacher wants" if teachers make marginal comments such as "You need more focus here" (Welch, 1998). Welch suggests a strategy she calls "sideshadowing," which she adapted from the theories of Morson and Bakhtin. She invites her students to turn in essays with their own marginal comments on them. Her responses, in turn, are reactions to their written essays, to their apparent intentions for the essay revealed in their marginal comments, and to the contemplations, conflicts, or decisions revealed in the students' marginal comments. In this way, both student and instructor see suggestions of what several different directions for revision might be, projected from the multiple perspectives on the writing. Revisions become more thoughtful, and the process reflects more ownership and decision making (and learning about writing) for students than when students think only about the instructor's suggestions for improvement. Theoretically, even comments that instructors intend as open-ended invitations for students to think about revisions can be experienced by students as foreclosing their decisions and foreshadowing the "revision" to come (Welch, 1998).

Mathematics

The assessment of problem-solving is of major importance in mathematics. There are many types of problems, however, depending on the context. Engineers, businesspeople, scientists, and mathematicians encounter in their work different kinds of problems that require mathematical solutions. Therefore, selection of problems, the reasoning required to solve them, and the style of communicating results should depend on the purpose of the mathematics course and its goals for learning.

One of the best ways to assess how students actually solve problems is to ask them to explain their reasoning, that is, to write about their math (National Council, 1989; Stiggins, 1997). Some writing assignments for calculus classes (from the mathematics department Web site at Franklin and Marshall College) include interesting titles such as "The Case of the Dead Doornail," "The General Spore," and "The Case of the Fall From Grace" (Crannell, 1998; see also Crannell, 1994). What sets these assignments apart from some others is the "Checklist for Your Writing Project" that serves as both an assessment tool and a clear description for students of the achievement target they are aiming for (Crannell, 1994, 1998). In other words, the questions on the checklist describe the characteristics of a clear and well-reasoned explanation, beginning with a clear restatement of the problem to be solved and moving through explanations of all the steps to the solution (see Table 14). Restating a problem in one's own words is a recognized way for students to demonstrate comprehension and not merely memorization (Nitko, 1996). A second important feature of this checklist is that it is a tool for students' assessment of their own work as well as for the instructor's grading. This approach increases students' ownership of the material and motivation and therefore improves learning.

The NCTM (National Council of Teachers of Mathematics) Standards (1989) recognize the importance of developing students' "mathematical power"—that is, their abilities to explore mathematical ideas, reason mathematically, solve nonroutine problems, and communicate mathematical concepts, all with some degree of self-confidence. To that end, the council recommends instruction and assessments aimed at developing these skills. Such assessments would include multistep, partial-credit problems and explanations of mathematical reasoning used to solve the problems, most easily scored with a problem-solving rubric or with a checklist such as the one recommended by Crannell (1994, p. 201; 1998). One of Crannell's calculus students commented, "You

TABLE 14

Sample Checklist for a Mathematics Writing Project

Directions:
Please attach this page with a paper clip to your writing assignment when you turn it in. This list will be used by your instructor to grade your assignment and will be returned to you with comments. Keep a copy of your paper for your own reference. Please feel free to use this checklist as a guide for yourself while writing this assignment.

Does this paper:

1. Clearly (re)state the problem to be solved?
2. State the answer in a complete sentence that stands on its own?
3. Clearly state the assumptions underlying the formulas?
4. Provide a paragraph that explains how the problem will be approached?
5. Clearly label diagrams, tables, graphs, or other visual representations of the math (if they are indeed used)?
6. Define all variables used?
7. Explain how each formula is derived, or where it can be found?
8. Give acknowledgment where it is due?

In this paper:

9. Are the spelling, grammar, and punctuation correct?
10. Is the math correct?
11. Did the writer solve the question that was originally asked?

Comments:

Source: Crannell, 1998. Used with permission.

don't realize that you have a gap in understanding until you have to explain how to do it" (Crannell, 1994, p. 199).

Social Sciences

As with English and mathematics, work in the social sciences requires analysis and writing skills as well as a command of discipline-specific facts and concepts. Notwithstanding these similarities, social science assignments differ from English or math assignments because of the differing nature of the work. Social science work includes writing histories, writing policy analyses, and examining economic and social trends.

Analytical and writing skills should be developed from the beginning of study. For example, the learning goals for a 100-level course in Western civilization included mastery of the facts and concepts of European history from 1500 to 1800 and beginning skill development in historical argumentation (see Walvoord & Anderson, 1998). Following the implications of these learning goals, the professor organized both his instruction and his assessment to coordinate with them.

Exposure to facts and concepts was accomplished by requiring short written assignments for out-of-class reading. In this way, the instructor arranged that most of the students would come to class having been exposed to the same new information, freeing class time to work on the process of using the information, now summarized in the students' own writing, for developing and supporting historical arguments to answer such questions as "Was Louis XIV of France a good king?" To construct a course in this manner and do it well, the instructor must have a clear picture of the achievement target. Table 15 presents the professor's analysis of the skills his students needed to develop. Each skill has implications for instruction and for the performance tasks and scoring criteria to be used in assessment.

Students' self-evaluations remain an important principle of assessment in the social sciences. In a self-assessment strategy used with freshman- and sophomore-level European civilization classes and junior- and senior-level history of science classes, students reviewed their own analysis of primary sources and written research papers (Steffens, 1991). A simple three-question "self-conference sheet" could also be used in peer conferences. What makes the questions good and appropriate for self-assessment is that they match the task's intended learning outcomes. Students are asked to check whether they have clearly described a hypothesis or thesis and whether they can identify how a reader would understand what their thesis is, points that are central to actual research writing. These questions also match what the instructor will look for in his evaluation of the students' final papers, which will count in their grades. Follow-up questions, probes, and additional specific questions, general or tailored to specific assignments, are useful during the process of drafting and revising the research papers (Steffens, 1991).

Natural Sciences

In college science classes, in-class examinations continue to be a mainstay of student assessment (Moscovici & Gilmer,

TABLE 15

**Sample Analysis of History Skills Required
For an Argumentative Essay**

1. *Reading accurately* (including an accurate sense of chronological narrative). Students must be able to report accurately on what they have read. They must know, for example, that events in 1645 could not have caused events in 1641.

2. *Realizing that published works have authors,* including paying attention to authors' personalities, possible biases, and attempts to organize material for the reader. Students should know who wrote their textbooks and be aware of the major section and chapter headings in them.

3. *Perceiving and using standard analytical categories,* including political, social, economic, religious, and cultural factors often cited in explaining past events.

4. *Perceiving historical theses.* Students must be able to see that historians *argue* about the past. They debate, for example, whether or not absolutism was beneficial to the majority of the French subjects of Louis XIV.

5. *Using written sources as evidence.* Facts become evidence only when brought forward in relation to a thesis. Both primary sources (contemporary eyewitness) and secondary sources may be used to state or defend a historical thesis.

6. *Stating and defending a historical thesis.* Accurate and specific examples and evidence are key to this skill; authors of secondary sources may be used as models, which can be done in two stages: (a) defending a thesis selected by the instructor and (b) choosing one's own thesis.

7. *Defending a historical thesis against counterarguments.* Agreeing with one author of a secondary source is not enough; students need to say why they rejected carefully argued opposing views. Again, accurate and specific examples are the key.

Source: J. Breihan, cited in Walvoord & Anderson, 1998, p. 52. Used with permission.

1996; Tobias & Raphael, 1995), stemming, perhaps, from the fact that for many science courses, knowledge of a large number of facts and concepts has been considered the hallmark of mastery. Science faculty in fact have been observed to resist alternative methods of assessment (Moscovici & Gilmer, 1996), perhaps in part because development of alternative assessments is not the sort of work that counts as scholarly publication in the sciences (Tobias & Raphael, 1995). Scientists, it seems, rely on fewer and less reliable measures of students' achievement—if one considers student assessments the "measures" taken in the "study" of one's course instruction—than they would in the studies of the physical world for their scientific research (Tobias & Raphael, 1995).

Nevertheless, many science instructors are adjusting their examinations, unpublished and largely unshared, and some changes are more sound than others. The changes include all kinds of strategies for adjusting points and format (Tobias & Raphael, 1995). In general, these innovations will be helpful to the extent that they pass the criteria for valid indicators of achievement. For strategies that deal with allocating points, the proportion of points earned for demonstrating achievement of various knowledge, skill, and thinking targets when final grades are assigned must match the intended goals of instruction, both in content and in relative weight. For strategies that deal with an assessment format, the changes involved must allow the actual achievement the student demonstrates to be what was intended for the course's learning goals. Some formats tap recall more easily than reasoning or understanding, although this judgment is not a simple one. For example, a good in-class test item can call forth reasoning and demonstration of a student's understanding, while a bad take-home test item may simply require students to use the index of a textbook and transcribe an answer from the book to the test pages.

Laboratory work and original research is a mainstay of scientific disciplinary study. Walvoord and Anderson's *Effective Grading* (1998) includes a running example from Anderson's biology classes. In a senior biology course, she assigns a research project in which students must "compare two commercially available products on the basis of at least four criteria to determine which is the 'better' product as operationally defined" (p. 39). This assignment directly relates to a goal for the course that students will be able to design, conduct, and communicate the results of original research as well as to a larger purpose many of her students have for taking the course—that they will soon be hired by companies

. . . a good in-class test item can call forth reasoning and demonstration of a student's understanding, while a bad take-home test item may simply require students to use the index of a textbook and transcribe an answer from the book to the test pages.

for which they would perform this kind of work. Thus, students' performance on the assignment may be expected to indicate in a valid manner their level of achievement.

The scoring criteria developed for the assignment use the principle that the scoring criteria and descriptors at the various levels on the rubrics themselves embody the characteristics of high-quality work (Stiggins, 1997). The reader is encouraged to look in more detail at the assignment and its rubrics. Good instruction and good assessment mingle in this example, and the result is amusing as well as uplifting. Students who apply Anderson's rubrics for a good report title, for example, find that "The Battle of the Suds" does not pass muster, while "A Comparison of Arizona and Snapple Iced Tea for pH, Residue, Light Absorbency, and Taste" does (Walvoord & Anderson, 1998, pp. 70-71).

Summary

Assessment in the disciplines relies on the previously described general principles for ensuring that assessment information is meaningful, useful for its intended purpose, and accurate. Its toolbox includes the paper-and-pencil test, performance assessment, oral question, and portfolio options. Differences in assessment among the disciplines stem from the fact that real work differs among the disciplines and from its corollary that the goals of learning for a course differ among the disciplines. This section has provided some examples of how the general principles for assessment apply in English, mathematics, social sciences, and natural sciences.

GRADING

This section takes up the first of two general questions about grading: How can the results of several different assessments be meaningfully combined into one composite grade for a course? (The second, about whether grade inflation exists and, if so, what can be done about it, is addressed in the next section.) Grading is a way to report or communicate information about a student's achievement in a course. The next subsection briefly explores ways to communicate students' achievement, and the following three offer information for instructors who wish (or need) to compute course grades as composites of the kinds of assessments discussed in the previous four sections.

Ways to Communicate Students' Achievement

All sorts of good reasons exist to communicate with students about their achievement. Grading is the most formal, constituting what has been called "official assessment" (Airasian, 1994). Instructors often wish to communicate with their students throughout the learning process, providing formative feedback or information students can use to monitor their progress, understand where they still need work, and improve their performance. Informational feedback that helps students improve their own work, not merely communicate a judgment like "fair," helps with students' motivation because it places a tool for improvement in their own hands. Formative assessments need not be part of official assessments; that is, it is not necessary to record a grade for every assignment students do. But homework problems and other formative assessments should be checked. It is not enough to simply note that the homework was completed.

The score on homework and other formative assessments need not be recorded if the intent of an assignment is practice and formative assessment. Doing an assignment for which the score does not count in the final grade allows students to *practice* and make genuine mistakes so they can see where more study is needed. But an assignment that does not count in the final grade may also send a message to students that the assignment is not very important. How students perceive the importance of work that does not count in a final grade depends on several factors, including how clear it is that the assignment provides valuable practice on important learning outcomes, the level of students' intellectual development and views of the purposes of education

(Perry, 1970), and the assessment environment in the classroom the instructor has created (Stiggins & Conklin, 1992).

Formative assessment and feedback are important for learning to occur (Black, 1998). Summative assessments provide overviews or summaries of previous learning (Black, 1998). Course grades, then, are summative assessments. Given the structure of college courses, the formative and summative functions of interim assignments blur. Any course assignment whose feedback students use to improve further work is functioning as formative assessment. Yet retrospectively from the end of the course, information from some of these formative assessments may be appropriate to select for construction of an overall indicator of students' achievement—namely, the grade.

Grading homework and other interim assignments must be kept at a manageable level, especially for large classes (see Walvoord & Anderson, 1998, for several good suggestions). One strategy is to develop simple rubrics for evaluating assignments; not every assignment requires written comments. Another strategy is to grade assignments on one particular criterion—for example, support of an argument appropriate to the lesson for which it was assigned—and ignore other possible criteria. A third strategy, important for its instructional and motivational utility as well as its efficiency, is to make good use of checklists, reflection, and other strategies for students' and their peers' assessment of the work.

Another useful way to communicate with students about their achievement is in a conference, either individually with the student or in small groups. Students may make appointments on their own initiative with an instructor outside class time to see how they are doing. An instructor may also wish to schedule student conferences as part of a course, either during or outside class time, to provide feedback about students' work.

Yet another way to communicate with students about their work is written feedback on papers, projects, or other assignments, either in addition to or in place of a grade. If this feedback is to be informative for students and useful for future improvement, it needs to do just that—give information (Ryan, Connell, & Deci, 1985). A comment like "good job" does not help the student as much as a comment telling why the job was good—for example, "good explanation of the poet's imagery." A grade of B does not help the student understand what would be needed for an A—for example,

"This essay does a good job of contrasting Ahab's and Ishmael's points of view. The essay would be stronger if you used these arguments to conclude what point(s) you think Melville is trying to make as an author."

Course Grades and the Nature of Composite Scores

Course grades usually require combining several individual grades into one. Several different valid methods can be used to aggregate grades on a set of course assignments into a student's course grade. The method should depend on the kind of assessment information available, which in turn should depend on the decisions about purpose and kind of scoring discussed in the preceding four sections, and on the kind of information the grade is intended to convey.

If a grade is meant to indicate achievement of a learning goal for the course that is an end-state result, such as writing a certain kind of research report, and not an average over a set of learning goals that were addressed one by one, then some kind of final performance grade, indexing the levels of skill with which students ended the course, is the best choice for a course grade. Students' practice work earlier in the semester, when they were developing skills and were free to make mistakes and to learn from them, should not count in the final grade. If a grade is meant to index a set of learning goals that were addressed over the course of a semester with various assessments, some kind of averaging makes sense. But be aware that some information is lost in any average. Averages mask variations in individual grades, so two different sets of grades (say, A,C,F and C,C,C) can end up with the same final average. Instructors should be sure, before they select an averaging method for calculating final grades, that overall performance on a set of learning goals measured with a set of assessments is what is called for.

If the purpose of each assignment is clear, if each assignment measures students' achievement on one or more learning goals for the course, and if the grade is intended to convey the sum or average of a set of achievements for the term, then a composite grade is in order. Putting grades together into a composite for a whole course is a matter of combining the scores on each assignment so that the relative weight they contribute to the final grade matches the instructor's intentions, the syllabus, and emphases communicated to students through the use of class time and instructional activities. When percentage of points earned on various assignments is the basis for assigning grades, the weight an assignment carries in the final grade depends on its total possible points. Using total possible points is consistent with a criterion-referenced approach to grading, in which students' work is compared with standards of performance and one student's grade does not depend on the grade of others.

When students' standing in the class is the basis for assigning grades, the weight an assignment carries in the final grade depends on the variability of scores. Students' performance on tests or assignments for which students all received similar scores does not affect students' standing (rank) for final grades as much as students' performance on tests or assignments on which scores varied widely. Using students' standing as the principle for assigning grades, a norm-referenced approach comparing students to one another, is not consistent with the learning-centered approach recommended in this monograph. As noted earlier, students prefer, value, and work harder for learning that is assessed by comparison with clear standards. The logic of an instructional model based on goals for learning also demands assessment by comparison with standards. The instructor's question in grading then becomes, "What portion of the achievement targets established as important in this course has each student attained?" Methods of assigning final grades described in this section are all compatible with a criterion- or learning-referenced approach to instruction and assessment. (See Oosterhof, 1987, or Ory & Ryan, 1993, for examples of how to weight scores for a norm-referenced, student-standing-based composite grade.)

As a "score" or measure, a course grade should be a measure of overall achievement or accomplishment of the learning goals for the course. Course grades should not be a proxy for general intelligence, a measure of effort or intentions, or any other non-achievement-related factor—partly because of the context of higher education, which to a certain extent is beyond instructors' choices or wishes. The result of whatever grading procedures are applied is a grade or mark, stored in the student's transcript next to the course title and number, for a number of years. Long after the instructor may have left the institution, the student will have Introduction to Western Civilization—B under his or her name. Whatever the instructor intended that B to mean, it will end up meaning "a B for achievement of whatever was taught in Introduction to Western Civilization."

Thus, the instructor's challenge is to use a method to combine the various achievement scores that are to count in the course grade in such a way that they give the most meaningful and accurate information one grade can convey about overall achievement for the course. To do so, the instructor must consider what relative weights the various components should have and use a method that does in fact allow the various components to carry those weights into the final composite grade.

Comparability of Scales

Tests or other assignments with grades that are added up as an accumulation of points or items correct, then calculated as a percentage of the total possible points, are said to be on an interval level scale. Thus, the space between each point or percentage is considered equal, and averaging is possible; that is, it is mathematically logical and defensible to add up the scores (or weighted scores) on different assignments and divide by the appropriate number to get a final average score. If the instructor has decided that a composite grade is appropriate for the course, the instructor's challenge for valid grading is in selecting a method of averaging that will give the intended weight for each assignment in the final average.

Percentages or points imply much more precise measurement than may really exist. For example, it may not be true that a student who scores 84% on the final exam really understands more of the course material or has demonstrated more thinking and reasoning skills with the material than a student who scores 83%.

Percentage or point scales also result in unequal grade ranges. Usually, the range for an F is very large, from 0 through 60% or 68%, and the ranges for A through D are 8, 9, or 10 points wide. When letter grades earned by finding the percentage of total possible points are recorded as letters, the implied 4-point scale (A = 4.00, B = 3.00, C = 2.00, D = 1.00, F = 0.00) no longer reflects these ranges.

Rubrics with very few points, like the holistic scale in Table 11, do not have the mathematical qualities that allow them to be meaningfully converted to percentages. Consider, for example, a 5-point rubric on which 5 is excellent performance with a description matching A-level work, 4 is good performance with a description matching B-level work, and so on. These rubric levels are rank-ordered levels that should not be converted to percentages. If an instructor mistakenly tries to do so, a score of 5 would end up as an A (5/5 = 100%), a 4 would be a B or C (4/5 = 80%) depending on the scale, and 3 or lower would be an F. The descriptions for the rubric levels would not match these grades; commonly, 3 would still describe acceptable work, and sometimes 2 would be passing as well. If a set has enough analytical rubrics so that the total possible points is 25 or 30, the instructor can total the rubric scores and then calculate percentage. While this method is not entirely satisfactory from a mathematical point of view, the results can be useful for grading.

What should be done when the course assignments are graded using a mixture of different kinds of scales? What if tests are graded using percentage correct, but projects and papers are graded using rubrics, for all the good reasons noted earlier? The principle involved is mathematical *precision,* the amount of detail that is actually present in a measure. Height is normally measured to the nearest inch, for example, and can be measured to the nearest half-inch. But it is not meaningful to say that someone is 64.3046 inches tall. It is simply not possible to measure height that precisely.

To make scales comparable, it is necessary to express all scores on the same scale. It is possible to collapse from more precision to less, but not the other way around. So, one way to combine percentage grades and rubric grades is to convert them all to letter grades, then use either the median or weighted letter grade approach to combining them (explained later) for the final grade. Percentages should be converted to grades in accordance with the policy that has already been communicated to students, either in the syllabus or in a handbook or institutional publication. Rubrics should be converted to grades in ways that are faithful to the meaning of the descriptions of the various levels of performance.

Sometimes institutional policy determines grade/percentage scales; other times instructors are free to choose their cutoff points. One example is 92–100 = A, 85–91 = B, 76–84 = C, 69–75 = D, 0–68 = F (Walvoord & Anderson, 1998). This scale has many variations, including the familiar 90–100 = A, 80–89 = B, 70–79 = C, 60–69 = D, 0–59 = F. Although these scales look very different, with the second one appearing much "easier" than the first, it is important to remember that these scales, and any institutional policy about them, beg the question "percent of what?" Ninety percent of a difficult assignment may be "harder" to achieve than 92% of a moderately easy assignment. Moreover, what is "easy" and "difficult" depends on the specific context and in part on a student's background and readiness to learn as well as the amount and quality of instruction the instructor has provided.

If the instructor intends to convert all results of assignments, whether percentages or rubrics, to grades, the rubric levels must be written with the grading scale in mind. If five different levels of distinction for the quality of students' work are needed for the final grade (A, B, C, D, and F), then a 4-point rubric is not precise enough, because it does not allow enough different distinctions. The instructor should decide before grading how many different quality levels he or she needs to distinguish and then write the rubric accordingly.

Methods for Combining Individual Scores Into Course Grades

Four methods for combining individual scores into course grades are presented here, with examples: the median method, weighted letter grades, total possible points, and holistic grading. They serve different purposes, depending on the course. In general, the weight of an individual grade is the portion it contributes to the final grade for the course. "Weight" is also used to mean a number an instructor might choose to multiply by an individual grade to change the portion it contributes to the final grade. For example, to double a score's contribution, multiply it by two. Two principles are important here. First, grades for individual assignments have weights relative to the final grade whether they have been adjusted by multiplication weighting methods or not. Second, if an individual assignment grade is multiplied by a weight to adjust its contribution to the final grade, the same procedure should be followed for all students.

Grading systems differ in the degree to which they are developmental, allowing early failure and practice, as opposed to unit based, where each unit is important (Walvoord & Anderson, 1998). The holistic method is particularly useful for courses where students work toward some final outcome and should not be penalized for their early work and practice. The median method is particularly appropriate when

Grading systems differ in the degree to which they are developmental, allowing early failure and practice, as opposed to unit based, where each unit is important.

individual students' performances vary widely over a semester, when scores are in grade or rubric form, or when grades are based on very few assignments.

Grading methods should be selected in conjunction with planning a course, so that the relative weights assigned to components of the grade match their coverage of intended learning goals in the same manner as the intentions for the course recorded on the syllabus. Weighted assignments should collectively index a "whole" that is a reasonable representation of achievement of intended course outcomes. Only a list of what each assessment represents can validate the choice of weights and demonstrate representation of learning outcomes. The lists of assessments without reference to content in the examples below are only for the purpose of illustrating calculations.

Median method
One way to calculate final grades for a course is to use the *median* of the set of individual assignment grades—that is, the value that falls in the middle of the scores when they are arranged in order from high to low, or vice versa, and counted. For example, the median of the set of grades A, C, and F is a C, and the median of the set of grades A, C, and D is also a C. The median is a good way to capture "typical" performance in a set of measures such as letter grades or rubrics. It is an excellent way to handle combining scores when some are grades from rubrics and some are grades from more precise scales that have been transformed to match.

For courses with a relatively small number of graded assignments, the median describes a student's typical or "average" achievement better than the mean or arithmetic average. Extreme scores, say one A or one F in an otherwise B-/C-level performance, do not pull the median as they would the mean or "average," thus giving students the freedom to do poorly on one performance without terrible damage to the overall grade. Some instructors allow for this occurrence in regular averaging by allowing students to choose one grade to ignore, but this method is unsatisfactory if the resulting final grade does not then represent all valued instructional intentions. When one grade is dropped, so is information about achievement on at least one learning goal for the course.

The median's property of not being unduly influenced by extreme grades is especially good for courses with very small numbers of grades, say a midterm, a final, and a paper. If there is one unusual performance among three, it is not possible to tell just how unusual it is. The extreme grade may even be more typical of the student than the other two.

In the median method, to weight an assignment double, simply enter the grade in the list twice. Suppose a student received an A on a final exam, a B on a paper, and a C on the midterm. Suppose further that the instructor wanted the final and the paper each to count twice as much as the midterm. This student's grade lineup, after weighting, would be A, A, B, B, C, and the median and final course grade would be a B, the middle in this array of five grades.

In the median method, if there are an even number of grades in the array, the median is the grade between the two middle grades. For example, the median of A, A, C, D is a B, halfway between the middle A and C, and the median of B, B, D, F is a C. The median of A, A, B, B is A- or B+, or if no minuses or pluses are allowed, the instructor would need to decide whether to round up to A or down to B.

Weighted letter grades
This method of calculating final grades uses the familiar scale A = 4.00, B = 3.00, C = 2.00, D = 1.00, F = 0.00. The system requires a decision when the course is planned about what percentage of the final grade each individual grade will be. The equation for calculation is as follows:

(Weight of grade 1)(Grade 1) + (Weight of grade 2)(Grade 2) + . . . + (Weight of grade n)(Grade n) = Final Grade

Table 16 illustrates this method and shows how two different students' final grades would be calculated.

Total possible points
The point approach to grading assigns a range of points to each component of the final grade. The example presented in Table 17 (Walvoord & Anderson, 1998, p. 94) uses the same relative weights as those in Table 16, and illustrates the impact of failing grades.

The final course grade is determined by the percentage scale set by the instructor or by department policy. This example uses the 90–100 = A scale. Table 17 illustrates the calculation of final grades with the total possible points method for

TABLE 16

The Weighted Letter Grade Method of Grading

Percentage of course grade	Student 1	Student 2
Test—average letter grade: 40%	B (3.00)	B (3.00)
Field project—letter grade: 30%	C (2.00)	F (0.00)
Final exam—letter grade: 20%	B (3.00)	B (3.00)
Class participation grade: 10%	B (3.00)	B (3.00)

Student 1's grade = (3)(.40) + (2)(.30) + (3)(.20) + (3)(.10) = 2.70 = B

Student 2's grade = (3)(.40) + (0)(.30) + (3)(.20) + (3)(.10) = 2.10 = C

the same two students, assuming their Bs and Cs were in the middle of the possible point range for these grades. Table 17 also illustrates the main difference between weighted letter grades and total possible points: the impact of an F. Recall that in the example, Student 2 failed the field project. In Table 17, Student 2's grade is calculated with a high F (57% of the 30 possible points for the field project) and a low F (27% of the 30 possible points for the field project). Notice that the difference between a high and a low F on the field project makes the difference between a C and a D for Student 2.

The point approach to grading accomplishes the same purpose as weighted letter grades, namely, to assign various weights to the assignments in the final grade that are proportional to their relative coverage of course outcomes. The difference, mathematically, is that for weighted letter grades, if the grades started as "percentage correct," then scaling has taken place before the final grade is calculated. It makes the most difference in the F range, as illustrated. Any F average for any of the components in the weighted letter grade system counts simply as zero, while the points received for an F in the points system can range from 0 through 60% (or whatever the cutoff is) of the total possible points.

If all grades on individual assignments are handled by assigning percentage scores, a variation of the total possible points approach will simplify calculations. Record everything in the grade book as a percent of 100, which puts all the grades on the same scale and, without further weighting, gives

TABLE 17

Total Possible Points Grading

	Student 1	Student 2 (high F)	Student 2 (low F)
Tests (out of 40 points)	34 (B)	34 (B)	34 (B)
Field project (30 points)	23 (C)	17 (F)	8 (F)
Final exam (20 points)	17 (B)	17 (B)	17 (B)
Class participation (10 points)	8 (B)	8 (B)	8 (B)
Total (final grade, out of 100 points)	82 (B)	76 (C)	67 (D)

them all the same weight in the final grade. A simple sum indicates how many hundreds of points describe the total. For example, if five assignments are all weighted equally, the course grade can be computed on the basis of 500 points. Weighting should be done before summing. In this example, if one of the assignments should be worth twice as much as the others, it should contribute 200 points, for a total of 600 for the course, and students' percentage scores on that assignment should be multiplied by 2 before being added in for the total.

The total possible points approach to grading means that the course has to be well planned in advance. The number and relative worth of assignments, and the resulting points for each assignment, must be established. A point system makes it difficult to adjust instruction and assessment based on students' needs or unsuccessful instruction. Therefore, a point system is recommended for courses that are fairly well established and have been demonstrated to run fairly consistently over time.

Grades as a holistic rating scale

Grades can be written as a holistic rating scale or rubric, constructed in the same fashion as scoring schemes for individual assignments, that is, with a description of the work required for each level. Walvoord and Anderson's (1998) "definitional system" for assigning grades amounts to a holistic scale. It assumes that each component of the grade is important in its own right and may not be averaged in with other work to compensate for it. Table 18 presents an example of a definitional system of grading. This system essen-

TABLE 18

A Definitional System for Grading a Course

To receive a particular course grade, you must meet or exceed the standards for each category of work. The following illustration shows a course with two distinct categories of work: graded work and pass-fail work.

Course grade	Graded work	Pass-fail work
A	A average	Pass for 90% or more of assignments
B	B average	Pass for 83% or more of assignments
C	C average	Pass for 75% or more of assignments
D	D average	Pass for 65% or more of assignments

Source: Walvoord & Anderson, 1998. Used with permission.

tially makes a rubric description for each grade level that specifies quantitatively what the minimal achievement levels are in two categories.

Another purpose of grading that a definitional system can serve is in the case when one main learning goal has formed the focus of a course, as may be particularly appropriate for upper-level courses that have as their major intended learning outcome a complex performance on some major project. For example, advanced seminars in a field often have as their major goal the student's synthesis of a body of literature, perhaps in a major paper. Research seminars often have as their main goal the design, implementation, and written description of some original research. Essentially, the grade for the course comes down to the grade for the major project, and it may best be described by spelling out the level of quality required. Table 19 presents an example for grading a literature review course.

A holistic, definitional scale such as the one in Table 19 could also be constructed for seminar courses in which discussion and debate are the main vehicles for dealing with the information. In that case, students' contributions of substance to the discussion, their preparation, and their considered responses to others would be the focus of the grading rubric.

A chapter on grading is included in the classic *Teaching Tips: Strategies, Research and Theory for College and University Teachers* (McKeachie, 1994); it cites a holistic grading rubric from 1950. Thus, the principle of establishing learning goals at the outset, distinguishing their relative importance,

TABLE 19

**A Grading Scale for an Advanced Seminar With a
Literature Review as Its One Major Goal**

Grade	
A	Major literature in the field has been located. Information is synthesized according to key principles or topics discussed in class or found in the literature. Reasonable conclusions have been drawn and are warranted from the results of the literature search. Writing is clear and readable.
B	Most major literature in the field has been located. Information is mainly synthesized by topic. Reasonable conclusions have been drawn and are warranted from the results of the literature search. Writing is clear and readable.
C	Some of the literature in the field has been located. Presentation may be list-like, reporting each piece of literature separately instead of synthesized by principle or topic. An attempt has been made to draw some conclusions from the list. Writing is mostly clear, although some points may be difficult to follow.
D	Some literature in the field has been located. Information is not organized. An attempt has been made to draw some conclusions, although the conclusions may not be supportable. Writing is not clear.
F	No literature is cited, or the literature cited is not relevant to the topic. Information is not organized. Writing is not clear.

and making grades reflect their accomplishment is not by any means a new recommendation:

A	*All major and minor goals achieved.*
B	*All major goals achieved; some minor ones not.*
C	*All major goals achieved; many minor ones not.*
D	*A few major goals achieved, but student is not prepared for advanced work.*
E or F	*None of the major goals achieved.* (Travers, cited in McKeachie, 1994, pp. 109-110)

Achievement of major and minor goals would need to be indicated by performance on various assessments keyed to the goals.

Summary
Instructors should choose the grading method that will result in grades that convey information about achievement of

learning goals for the course. It follows that two important considerations in choosing a grading method should be the nature of the course learning goals themselves—especially whether intended course learning outcomes comprise a set of several goals or one general developmental goal—and the nature of the individual assessments used to measure them. For courses with one general developmental goal, a holistic grading system is recommended. For courses with sets of learning goals that should be considered together in the final grade, the nature of individual assignment grades helps instructors determine an appropriate method for combining them. If only a few grades have been assigned, or if grades vary widely for individual students, the median method is recommended. If a fair number of grades are on point or percentage scales, the weighted letter grade or total possible point methods can be used.

GRADE DISTRIBUTIONS AND GRADING POLICIES

This section concentrates on literature about issues related to grading as a faculty activity: fairness, students' expectations, grade inflation, and grading policies. Most higher education institutions have grading policies. Almost all have policies about what grades may be given. Is plus/minus grading allowed? Is an A+ possible? Which courses may be taken as pass/fail? Which courses must be taken as pass/fail? How will pass/fail grades be figured into the grade point average? Some institutions have policies about grade point averages required for admission into, retention in, or graduation from a program. Some have policies that specify the percentage equivalents for various grades, although that does beg the question "percentage of what?"

The Literature on Grading: Course Planning and Student Results

Tables 20 and 21 present the results of the literature review specific to grading. Table 20 presents essays and other descriptive analyses, Table 21 empirical studies. Clearly, one issue that stands out in the current literature about grading in higher education is a concern about grade inflation (see the following subsection), but it is worth noting that although the concern in the current literature is grade inflation, grade deflation has also been reported as a problem in other periods during this century (Milton, Pollio, & Eison, 1986).

Another theme in this review is the principle that well chosen instructional goals, carefully planned syllabi, well executed classroom instruction, and high quality interactions with students are more important than the grades that result (Hammons & Barnsley, 1992; Walvoord & Anderson, 1998). After assignments have been turned in and the instructor is preparing to grade them, it is too late to start worrying about grades. The end of the term is certainly too late. Concern with "how students do" should begin at the beginning, when instruction is planned and the syllabus prepared.

Grade Inflation

"Grade inflation" describes the condition that exists when grades rise without accompanying gains in achievement. Conversely, "grade deflation" describes the condition that exists when grades fall without accompanying drops in achievement. If grades in a given program rise but students actually learned more, either because students in the pro-

TABLE 20

Essays About Grading in College Classrooms

Source	Topic	Main points
Basinger, 1997	Grade inflation masks other problems	• Grade inflation is sometimes seen as an indication that academic standards have declined, with the assumption that faculty know how to teach and assess well; former grade distributions may also be related to "harder" but equally misguided teaching, such as requiring a large amount of memorization of facts. • Instead of working on grade inflation, we should be working to ensure that appropriate content is selected, taught, and graded well. If a section receives high grades because they all achieved something, that's fine.
Brookhart, 1998	Grade inflation	• Factors behind grade inflation include external pressure, internal pressure, confusion of judge and advocate roles in education, and change in model of education from information-transmission to objectives-driven instruction. • Just holding firm addresses only external pressure.
Dreyfuss, 1993	Grade inflation	• Concerns about grade inflation mistakenly make the grade the object, when the object of education should be learning to think critically in a discipline. • Would prefer clear criteria and then 2-part written evaluations (student and faculty). • Keep in mind adult students' needs.
Hammons & Barnsley, 1992	Grading	• Brief history of grading • Defines 4 approaches to grading: norm, criterion, mastery, and pass/fail • Gives principles to use in selecting a grading plan
Mitchell, 1998	Grade variation	• Inflation is a problem, contrary to popular belief not linked to course evaluations (assertion as department chair), but between-section variation of grades is a more serious problem. • Need to establish clear criteria for performance and use grades to distinguish among levels of performance; discussion among faculty is a necessary first step but will not be sufficient to solve the problem.

TABLE 21

Empirical Studies of Grading in College Classrooms

Study	Context	Sample	Method	Findings
L. Cross, Frary, & Weber, 1993	Large research university	365 faculty	Survey of grading practices	• Most espouse absolute (versus relative) standards but don't always use methods accordingly. • Record letter grades, percentage scores, and points mostly (more often percentage for tests than for papers, projects, or homework) • Most penalize absence from an exam with an F for the exam. • Don't consider non-achievement factors much, except for borderline cases

gram were abler than before or because the instruction was better, that is not grade inflation.

Defining "grade inflation" in this way sidesteps a serious philosophical issue about the purpose of education and the relation between grading and the mission of schooling. Most schools no longer espouse a mission of ranking students but rather declare a mission of ensuring students' competence in reading, writing, problem solving, and the disciplines. Such a mission implies that instructors should not be satisfied with their teaching unless they can justifiably assign grades indicating a high level of competence for most of their students.

A review of studies of grade inflation and deflation (Milton, Pollio, & Eison, 1986) concluded that before the early 1970s, grade deflation was a concern. Two studies, one at the Women's College of the University of North Carolina and one at the University of California at Berkeley, found that in the late 1950s and early 1960s, SAT scores had risen but grade point averages remained stable. Beginning in the early 1970s, that trend reversed; studies from various schools reported rising grade point averages. Milton, Pollio, and Eison's analysis ended with 1980. They concluded that col-

TABLE 21 (continued)

Study	Context	Sample	Method	Findings
Stone, 1995	State of Tennessee	13,703 seniors from 29 Tennessee colleges and other institutional reports	Synthesis of data from several sources	• Grade inflation has led to enrollment inflation, which has led to budget inflation. • Study uses data from Tennessee but suggests it generalizes and recommends research in other states and at individual institutions. • Administrators not faculty run institutions; suggests faculty "know how to teach" but are constrained from doing so.
Summerville, Ridley, & Maris, 1990	Small college	Survey of 116 urban/ suburban institutions using grade records from 1967-1976 and college database from 1979-1986	Plotted grades over time; compared grades for students taking courses in their department with the same students' grades while simultaneously enrolled in other departments	• Grade inflation occurred at the college. • Serious local departmental differences in grading • For 39 institutions providing departmental data, on average 3 times as much variability between departments as between years
Walhout, 1997	40-year teaching career from 1952-1992	4,969 students	Gives career grade distribution and grade averages by career decades	• Has a C+ overall career average; discusses in light of current concerns for grade inflation

lege grades differed with expectations for different eras and that grades simply do not have a fixed value over time.

An analysis of grade distributions and ACT scores for students in higher education in Tennessee from 1965 to 1991 (Stone, 1995) concluded that the overall grade distribution in the state had shifted up 0.5 (on the 4-point grading scale

where A = 4.0) such that about 15% of 1991 college gradu-
ates in Tennessee would not have graduated in 1965. Stone
argued that the "lowered standards" apparent in this grade
inflation were largely the result of enrollment-driven funding
and administrative priorities that worked against holding
students to rigorous academic standards.

Summerville, Ridley, and Maris (1990) found evidence of
grade inflation from 1967 through 1986. They studied an un-
named institution in detail and surveyed peer institutions for
benchmark information. Although they found evidence of
grade inflation, they found that differences in grading
among academic departments were far more dramatic and,
in their view, cause for greater concern. Because students'
grades from across university departments are convention-
ally averaged to compute grade point averages, even "grade
inflation" figures actually mask the variability in grades. And
to the extent that grades are not comparable from course to
course, it does not make mathematical sense to average
them—calling into question the meaning of the ubiquitous
grade point average.

Thus, the studies reveal at least two different approaches
to grade inflation: considering it a serious general problem or
considering it camouflage for the more serious problem of the
apparent comparability of achievement levels from course to
course that grades imply. Four issues underlie the problem of
grade inflation: external pressure, internal pressure from instructors on themselves, a confusion of the roles of judge and
advocate in our educational system, and a change in the mission of education and model of instruction whose effects the
grades are designed to measure (Brookhart, 1998).

External pressure is the common notion that in a higher
education market increasingly driven by consumers' needs
and wishes, instructors are under pressure from students and
parents to give high grades. The emotional tone in some of
the literature reviewed here testifies to the fact that some instructors do feel this pressure. The entertainment-style approach to education—that is, breaking down difficult concepts into small bites that "anyone" can swallow—is a mixed
blessing, however. A fine line exists between accepting any
old work and honoring anyone's work, and educators are
more and more pressed to draw that line as more and more
consumers buy into higher education. Where and how to
draw that line is a negotiable issue.

. . . "lowered standards" apparent in this grade inflation were largely the result of enrollment-driven funding and administrative priorities that worked against holding students to rigorous academic standards.

Internal pressure refers to the fact that many instructors dislike grading (Hammons & Barnsley, 1992), especially because they want to encourage their students. Some do not fail students who "try," or who at least are perceived to be trying. This reluctance to fail students suggests the third issue, confusion of the role of judge and advocate in the educational system. The same instructor who is the teacher, the coach, the guide, the advocate "for" the student, must turn around and judge the student. In a court of law or on the playing field, this culture separates judges and advocates, referees and coaches. But in education the same person must fulfill both functions. It is a difficult task made even more difficult by the fact that the function of advocacy is more closely related to the reasons people give for becoming educators in the first place—to help students learn and grow—than is the function of judgment. So the instructor's motivation to judge or grade is less compelling than the motivation to help, to guide, to coach, to teach.

The fourth issue behind grade inflation is a change in the nature of the educational mission and the population it serves. As more and more people need and want to attend institutions of higher education, it is less and less useful to "sort" people based on passing and failing and more and more important to ensure that students can attain specified levels of achievement. The information-transmission model of education, in which the student's job is to receive information, has given way to a goal-driven model of instruction, in which the instructor is seen as responsible for specifying learning goals for his or her classes, arranging instructional activities aimed at students' progress toward those goals, and then assessing the outcome. Short of misbehavior or intentionally ignoring instruction, most students who are given objectives and the means to meet them will do so. The resulting grade distribution will not be a normal curve, with most people scoring a C, but a skewed distribution with an average grade of B.

Summary

Faculty who clearly understand student assessment can both communicate and measure their expectations for students. Thus, faculty can foster students' success without lowering standards. The literature suggests that concern over grade inflation is widespread and that grade inflation may be tied to political and funding pressures on institutions as much as to individual students' pressure on their instructors. The literature also suggests, however, that an excessive focus on grade inflation at the aggregated level (grade point average) diverts educators' attention from the more important matter of the meaning and soundness of individual course grades and the quality of classroom teaching and learning.

CONCLUSIONS AND FURTHER RESOURCES FOR FACULTY

Conclusions

The intent of this monograph is to provide college and university instructors with a working knowledge of classroom assessment principles and an overview of the literature about classroom assessment in higher education. Assessment means gathering and interpreting information about students' achievement of the learning goals for a course. Assessment of students serves several important purposes in higher education: feedback to students about their progress, information upon which to base grades for the course, and evaluation of programs.

Each of the four ways of measuring achievement of course objectives discussed—paper-and-pencil tests, performance assessments, oral questions, and portfolios—is particularly well suited to collecting useful information for instructors and students about different kinds of achievement, including knowledge, thinking skills, procedural skills, projects and products, and dispositions. Scoring any of these forms of assessment may be objective (right/wrong answers or yes/no to items on a checklist) or subjective (judgments of gradations of quality) (see "Options for Classroom Assessment" for how to construct and score the various kinds of assessments).

Because assessment of students provides information to support students' motivation and learning and to monitor instruction, it is vital that information gleaned from assessment be meaningful and appropriate (valid) and accurate and dependable (reliable). To ensure the quality of such information, match assessment methods to the course's learning goals, write clear and unambiguous tests, directions, and assignments, and make sure the scoring and weighting of results match intended goals for the course. Scores should be intended for a particular purpose, and they should be accurate. Combining scores from several different assessments into meaningful course grades requires planning. Attention must be given to the weighting of various scores that go into the grade and to their method of combination so that the final grade reflects the relative emphasis of intended goals for the course.

A relatively larger amount of classroom assessment literature has been written for K–12 education than for higher education, and although the principles for good classroom assessment remain the same for both levels, this monograph concentrates on assessment for college courses and young (and not-so-young) adult students. If anything, the higher education context underscores the importance of fairness and clarity in tests, assignments, and scoring and of clear descriptions of achievement targets or learning goals. Today, when a wide variety of students attend college, learning should be more of a concern than grading. It is not a matter of flunking out those who do not belong in higher education; rather, it is a matter of helping each student achieve the level he or she is capable of. Good assessment provides students the feedback they need to monitor their progress and provides the instructor a vehicle through which to fairly grade students' achievement.

Few empirical studies of classroom assessment in higher education have been completed. A much greater proportion of the assessment literature for higher education is focused on institutional assessment of outcomes and on anonymous classroom assessment techniques that provide feedback for the instructor than on classroom assessment of individual students' achievement. Although all three functions are important, more studies are needed that investigate the needs, types, results, and effectiveness of assessment in the higher education classroom.

Also needed is more professional development in assessment geared toward higher education instructors. The preparation and experience of most college professors has been largely disciplinary; the methods of education are not part of their training. In particular, assessment in higher education is often treated as part of academic freedom or the instructor's prerogative. But instructors who attend to assessment have reported their results to be good and have increased both students' learning and their own excitement about their teaching. When instructors can see evidence of students' learning and have confidence that their evidence is solid, both students and instructors benefit.

Further Resources

Higher education instructors who are convinced by the argument of this monograph that assessment of students' achievement in university courses is a crucial teaching function and a professional responsibility may wish to pursue professional development in classroom assessment. The following paragraphs identify such resources.

Course planning and grading

Effective Grading (Walvoord & Anderson, 1998) contains some excellent suggestions for grading. It begins at the beginning, however, with course planning, and suggests that the assessments and instruction be planned to match the professor's instructional intent for the course and that the syllabus clearly communicate these intentions to students. Grading is a natural extension of good instruction, communicating the total of a semester's worth of achievement.

This resource is recommended first in this section because, of all the resources surveyed, it is the single best source. It is comprehensive and clear, and its themes and examples are all consistent with principles of sound instruction and sound assessment. It is written with a wealth of examples from higher education across a wide variety of disciplines: art history, biology, business, dental hygiene, English, mathematics, to name a few. Its approach to grading is criterion referenced. The authors are themselves both college professors. If only one additional resource on assessment of students in higher education could be recommended, it would be this one.

Writing good tests

Many educational measurement and classroom assessment textbooks give good, clear, extended treatment of writing test items. Recommended in particular are *Educational Assessment of Students* (Nitko, 1996), especially good for its excellent treatment of writing and scoring essay questions, and *Measurement and Assessment in Teaching* (Linn & Gronlund, 1995), especially good for its treatment of writing multiple-choice questions. The intended audience for these texts includes teachers at all grade levels, but readers will find the examples applicable to college level study. Other helpful textbooks on classroom assessment include *Student-Centered Classroom Assessment* (Stiggins, 1997) and *Educational Testing and Measurement* (Kubiszyn & Borich, 1993). *Tips for Improving Testing and Grading* (Ory & Ryan, 1993) is intended for higher education faculty.

Instructors who regularly teach the same courses may save time and increase the validity and variety of test questions if they develop an "item bank," that is, a database of test questions, indexed by topic and sometimes by level of thinking. Although item banks can be stored in paper files,

Instructors who regularly teach the same courses may save time and increase the validity and variety of test questions if they develop an "item bank," that is, a database of test questions . . .

usually the term refers to a computer file produced with item banking software. Once written and indexed, items can be stored and used in various combinations for different tests, year after year. A good introductory resource for instructors who wish to learn more about item banking is "Guidelines for the Development of Item Banks" (Ward & Murray-Ward, 1994).

Designing performance assessments

An excellent how-to article about designing performance assessments based on observation and judgment of the process or products of students' work is "Design and Development of Performance Assessments" (Stiggins, 1987), an instructional module published by the National Council on Measurement in Education (NCME). Stiggins's text (1997) is also an excellent source of information on this topic. Again, examples from basic education would not be hard to extend to higher education. Other NCME instructional modules that might be helpful include "Assessing Student Achievement With Term Papers and Written Reports" (Brookhart, 1993) and "Using Portfolios of Student Work in Instruction and Assessment" (Arter & Spandel, 1992). *A Practical Guide to Alternative Assessment* (Herman, Aschbacher, & Winters, 1992) is a short, readable book that functions just as its title suggests, while *Strategies for Diversifying Assessment in Higher Education* (S. Brown, Rust, and Gibbs, 1994) is a workbook-style presentation that is aimed specifically at higher education classrooms.

The Northwest Regional Educational Laboratory (NWREL) publishes a wonderful resource for those who must plan and lead faculty development in alternative assessment. The two editions of *A Toolkit for Professional Developers* (1994, 1998) include plans for workshop sessions of varying lengths in all aspects of alternative assessment. In addition, NWREL has a comprehensive and helpful Web site with a large amount of space devoted to assessment (http://www.nwrel.org).

Colleagues

Higher education faculty sometimes miss out on the opportunity to talk with colleagues and share ideas. The nature of the job makes scheduling, meeting, and simply finding time somewhat difficult. But some of the most interesting and useful information comes from sharing ideas that worked—and those that did not—with colleagues.

On many campuses, faculty can turn to local university exam services for technical help in developing assessments, scoring them, and analyzing their quality. Readers are encouraged to find out what services are available on their own campuses.

Other resources

Several resources include some ideas that could be adapted to classroom assessment of individual students' achievement in higher education, even though it is not their primary purpose. Sometimes these "sources of inspiration" are very important, because they stretch the faculty member's mind and stimulate original thinking about course content, the students, and the context of the class.

One such resource is *Classroom Assessment Techniques: A Handbook for College Teachers* (Angelo and Cross, 1993). These techniques are intended for assessment of a group's understanding of classroom lessons and are intended to be administered anonymously. But the pages contain a wealth of ideas, many of which can be successfully adapted to nonanonymous student assessment of course achievement for credit. Other classroom assessment techniques could be adapted and modified to be suitable for nonanonymous student assessment.

Another resource is the American Association for Higher Education's *Learning Through Assessment: A Resource Guide for Higher Education* (Gardiner, Anderson, & Cambridge, 1997), a compilation of resources, including a large annotated bibliography on assessment. Its focus is institutional assessment and program evaluation, so its concern is more standardized assessment at levels aggregated beyond the classroom. Some of the general resources, however, are useful in classrooms.

A good source of ideas about classroom assessment comes in the periodicals targeted to college teaching. Sometimes such journals include articles about assessment; sometimes they include articles about instruction that an assessment-literate instructor can see have implications for assessment. Journals addressing general college teaching include *College Teaching* and *Journal on Excellence in College Teaching*.

Discipline-specific teaching journals are good sources of instructional and assessment strategies suitable to individual disciplines. Often, they are published by professional organizations in the field. Some include suggestions for both high school and college classrooms. Such journals are highly recommended as a source of interesting, novel, and discipline-appropriate ideas.

In sum, readers are encouraged not to stop here. Instead, they are urged to think about ways that the ideas in this review apply to courses they teach, to try various strategies of assessment, and reflect on the results. And they are encouraged to consult the resources offered here for further study.

REFERENCES

The Educational Resources Information Center (ERIC) Clearing-house on Higher Education abstracts and indexes the current litera-ture on higher education for inclusion in ERIC's database and an-nouncement in ERIC's monthly bibliographic journal, *Resources in Education* (RIE). Most of these publications are available through the ERIC Document Reproduction Service (EDRS). For publications cited in this bibliography that are available from EDRS, ordering number and price code are included. Readers who wish to order a publication should write to the ERIC Document Reproduction Ser-vice, 7420 Fullerton Road, Suite 110, Springfield, Virginia 22153-2852. (Phone orders with VISA or MasterCard are taken at (800) 443-ERIC or (703) 440-1400.) When ordering, please specify the document (ED) number. Documents are available as noted in mi-crofiche (MF) and paper copy (PC). If you have the price code ready when you call, EDRS can quote an exact price. The last page of the latest issue of *Resources in Education* also has the current cost, listed by code.

Airasian, P. W. (1994). *Classroom assessment* (2nd ed.). New York: McGraw-Hill.

American Federation of Teachers, National Council on Measure-ment in Education, & National Education Association. (1990). *Standards for teacher competence in educational assessment of students*. Washington, DC: Author. ED 323 186. 7 pp. MF–01; PC–01.

Angelo, T. A., & Cross, K. P. (1993). *Classroom assessment tech-niques: A handbook for college teachers* (2nd ed.). San Francisco: Jossey-Bass.

Arter, J., & Spandel, V. (1992). Using portfolios of student work in instruction and assessment. *Educational Measurement: Issues and Practice, 11*(1), 36-44.

Arter, J., Spandel, V., & Culham, R. (1995). Portfolios for assessment and instruction. *ERIC Digest*. Available: http://ericae.net/db/edo/ED388890.htm. ED 388 890. 4 pp. MF 01; PC–01.

Basinger, D. (1997). Fighting grade inflation: A misguided effort? *College Teaching, 45*(3), 88-91.

Bennett, R. E. (1993). On the meanings of constructed response. In R. E. Bennett & W. C. Ward (Eds.), *Construction versus choice in cognitive measurement*. Hillsdale, NJ: Erlbaum.

Black, P. (1998). *Testing: Friend or foe?* London: Falmer Press.

Brookhart, S. M. (1993). Assessing student achievement with term papers and written reports. *Educational Measurement: Issues and Practice, 12*(1), 40-47.

Brookhart, S. M. (1997, March). *The relationship of classroom as-sessment to student effort and achievement in the college class-*

room: Pilot study technical report. Paper presented at the annual meeting of the American Educational Research Association, Chicago, IL.

Brookhart, S. M. (1998). Why "grade inflation" is not a problem with a "just say no" solution. *National Forum, 78*(2), 3-5.

Brown, B. S. (1994, March). The grade effect of re-using examination questions: A case study. *College Student Journal, 28,* 77-81.

Brown, S., Rust, C., & Gibbs, G. (1994). *Strategies for diversifying assessment in higher education.* Oxford, Eng.: Oxford Centre for Staff Development.

Buchanan, R. W., & Rogers, M. (1990). Innovative assessment in large classes. *College Teaching, 38*(2), 69-73.

Community College of Vermont. (1992). *Teaching for development: A handbook for instructors.* Waterbury, VT: Author. ED 341 446. 70 pp. MF–01; PC–03.

Covington, M. V. (1992). *Making the grade.* Cambridge, Eng.: Cambridge University Press.

Crannell, A. (1994). How to grade 300 mathematical essays and survive to tell the tale. *PRIMUS, 4*(3), 193-204.

Crannell, A. (1998). Writing in mathematics. Web site, Franklin & Marshall College. Available: http://www.fandm.edu/Departments/Mathematics/writing_in_math/writing_index.html.

Cross, K. P., & Angelo, T. A. (1988). *Classroom assessment techniques: A handbook for faculty.* Ann Arbor, MI: National Center for Research to Improve Postsecondary Teaching and Learning. ED 317 097. 166 pp. MF–01; PC–07.

Cross, L. H., Frary, R. B., & Weber, L. J. (1993). College grading: Achievement, attitudes, and effort. *College Teaching, 41*(4), 143-148.

Crouch, M. K., & Fontaine, S. I. (1994). Student portfolios as an assessment tool. In D. Halpern (Ed.), *Changing college classrooms: New teaching and learning strategies for an increasingly complex world* (pp. 306-328). San Francisco: Jossey-Bass.

Dreyfuss, S. (1993). My fight against grade inflation. *College Teaching, 41*(4), 149-152.

Gardiner, L. F., Anderson, C., & Cambridge, B. L. (Eds.) (1997). *Learning through assessment: A resource guide for higher education.* AAHE Assessment Forum. Washington, DC: American Association for Higher Education. ED 414 814. 118 pp. MF–01; PC not available EDRS.

Glasgow, J. N. (1993). Portfolio portrait and assessment. *Issues and Inquiry in College Learning and Teaching, 16*(2), 57-74.

Guthrie, D. S. (1992). Faculty goals and methods of instruction:

Approaches to classroom assessment. In *Assessment and curriculum reform* (pp. 69-80). New Directions for Higher Education No. 80. San Francisco: Jossey-Bass.

Hackett, M. S., & Levine, J. R. (Eds.). (1993, March). *Teaching of psychology: Ideas and innovations.* Proceedings of the seventh annual conference on undergraduate teaching of psychology, Ellenville, NY. ED 365 398. 170 pp. MF–01; PC–07.

Hale, M. E., Shaw, E. L., Burns, J. C., & Okey, J. R. (1984, April). *Development of a computer animated science process skills test.* Paper presented at the annual meeting of the National Association for Research in Science Teaching, New Orleans, LA. ED 248 111. 12 pp. MF–01; PC–01.

Hammons, J. O., & Barnsley, J. R. (1992). Everything you need to know about developing a grading plan for your course (well, almost). *Journal on Excellence in College Teaching, 3,* 51-68.

Harris, O. D. (1994). Equity in classroom assessment. In H. Roberts, J. Gonzales, O. Harris, D. Huff, A. Johns, R. Lou, & O. Scott (Eds.), *Teaching from a multicultural perspective.* Thousand Oaks, CA: Sage.

Herman, J. L., Aschbacher, P. R., & Winters, L. (1992). *A practical guide to alternative assessment.* Alexandria, VA: ASCD.

Jacobsen, R. H. (1993). What is good testing? Perceptions of college students. *College Teaching, 41*(4), 153-156.

Joint Advisory Committee. (1993). Principles for fair student assessment practices for education in Canada. Edmonton, Alberta: Author.

Joint Committee on Standards for Educational Evaluation. (1998). Student evaluation standards: Descriptors and standard statements. Kalamazoo, MI: The Evaluation Center, Western Michigan University.

Kubiszyn, T., & Borich, G. (1993). *Educational testing and measurement* (4th ed.) New York: HarperCollins.

Lantos, G. (1992). Evaluating written work: You get what you expect. *Issues and Inquiry in College Learning and Teaching, 15*(3), 79-86.

Larson, A. M. (1995). *Portfolio assessment of student achievement at baccalaureate colleges II for classroom and institutional accountability decisions.* Ph.D. dissertation, University of Nebraska–Lincoln.

Liggett, S. (1986, March). *Learning to grade papers.* Paper presented at the annual meeting of the Conference on College Composition and Communication, New Orleans, LA. ED 270 814. 21 pp. MF–01; PC–01.

Linn, R. L., & Gronlund, N. (1995). *Measurement and assessment in teaching* (7th ed.). Englewood Cliffs, NJ: Merrill.

McClymer, J. F., & Knoles, L. Z. (1992). Ersatz learning, inauthentic testing. *Journal on Excellence in College Teaching, 3,* 33-50.

McKeachie, W. J. (1994). *Teaching tips: Strategies, research and theory for college and university teachers* (9th ed.). Lexington, MA: D. C. Heath.

McTighe, J., & Ferrara, S. (1994, November). *Assessing learning in the classroom.* Washington, DC: National Education Association. ED 393 870. 35 pp. MF–01; PC not available EDRS.

Messick, S. (1989). Meaning and values in test validation: The science and ethics of assessment. *Educational Researcher, 18*(2), 5-11.

Milton, O., Pollio, H. R., & Eison, J. A. (1986). *Making sense of college grades.* San Francisco: Jossey-Bass.

Mitchell, L. C. (1998, May 8). Inflation isn't the only thing wrong with grading. *Chronicle of Higher Education,* A72.

Moscovici, H., & Gilmer, P. J. (1996, March/April). Testing alternative assessment strategies: The ups and the downs for science-teaching faculty. *Journal of College Science Teaching, 25,* 319-323.

Munson, S. (1995). GSPED 662, learning disabilities. Unpublished syllabus. Pittsburgh, PA: Duquesne University.

Murray, J. P. (1990). Better testing for better learning. *College Teaching, 38*(4), 148-152.

National Council of Teachers of Mathematics. (1989). *Curriculum and evaluation standards for school mathematics.* Reston, VA: Author.

Nitko, A. J. (1996). *Educational assessment of students* (2nd ed.). Englewood Cliffs, NJ: Merrill.

Northwest Regional Educational Laboratory. (1994, November). *A toolkit for professional developers: Alternative assessment.* Portland, OR: Author.

Northwest Regional Educational Laboratory. (1998, February). *Improving classroom assessment: A toolkit for professional developers.* Portland, OR: Author.

O'Keefe, R. D. (1996). Comment codes: Improving turnaround time for student reports. *College Teaching, 44*(4), 137-138.

Oosterhof, A. J. (1987). Obtaining intended weights when combining student scores. *Educational Measurement: Issues and Practice, 6*(4), 29-37.

Ory, J., & Ryan, K. (1993). *Tips for improving testing and grading.* Newbury Park, CA: Sage.

O'Sullivan, R. G., & Johnson, R. L. (1993). *Using performance assessments to measure teachers' competence in classroom assessment.* Paper presented at the annual meeting of the American Educational Research Association, Atlanta, GA. ED 358 156. 22 pp. MF–01; PC–01.

Perry, W. G. (1970). *Forms of intellectual and ethical development in the college years: A scheme.* New York: Holt, Rinehart & Winston.

Platt, L., Turocy, P., & McGlumphy, B. (1998, Spring). Final exam: Art and Science II. Pittsburgh, PA: Department of Athletic Training, Duquesne University.

Rodabaugh, R. C., & Kravitz, D. A. (1994). Effects of procedural fairness on student judgments of professors. *Journal on Excellence in College Teaching, 5*(2), 67-83.

Ryan, R. M., Connell, J. P., & Deci, E. L. (1985). A motivational analysis of self-determination and self-regulation in the classroom. In C. Ames & R. Ames (Eds.), *Research on motivation in education: Vol. 2, The classroom milieu.* Orlando, FL: Academic Press.

San Diego County Office of Education. (1998). Web page design rubric. Available: http://www.sdcoe.k12.ca.us/score/actbank/WebPageDesign.html.

Snow, R. E. (1993). Construct validity and constructed-response tests. In R. E. Bennett & W. C. Ward (Eds.), *Construction versus choice in cognitive measurement.* Hillsdale, NJ: Erlbaum.

Stearns, S. A. (1996). Collaborative exams as learning tools. *College Teaching, 44*(3), 111-112.

Steffens, H. (1991). Helping students improve their own writing: The self-conference sheet. *The History Teacher, 24*(2), 239-241.

Stiggins, R. J. (1987). Design and development of performance assessments. *Educational Measurement: Issues and Practice, 6*(3), 33-42.

Stiggins, R. J. (1992). High quality classroom assessment: What does it really mean? *Educational Measurement: Issues and Practice, 11*(2), 35-39.

Stiggins, R. J. (1997). *Student-centered classroom assessment* (2nd ed.). Upper Saddle River, NJ: Merrill.

Stiggins, R. J., & Conklin, N. F. (1992). *In teachers' hands: Investigating the practices of classroom assessment.* Albany, NY: SUNY Press.

Stone, J. E. (1995). Inflated grades, inflated enrollment, and inflated budgets: An analysis and call for review at the state level. *Education Policy Analysis Archives 3*(11). Available: http://olam.ed.asu.edu/epaa/v3n11.html.

Summerville, R. M., Ridley, D. R., & Maris, T. L. (1990). Grade inflation: The case of urban colleges and universities. *College Teaching, 38*(1), 33-38.

Tobias, S., & Raphael, J. (1995, February). In-class examinations in college science: New theory, new practice. *Journal of College Science Teaching, 24,* 242-244.

Walhout, D. (1997). Grading across a career. *College Teaching, 45*(3), 83-87.

Walvoord, B. E., & Anderson, V. J. (1998). *Effective grading: A tool for learning and assessment.* San Francisco: Jossey-Bass.

Ward, A. W., & Murray-Ward, M. (1994). Guidelines for the development of item banks. *Educational Measurement: Issues and Practice, 13*(1), 34-39.

Welch, N. (1998). Sideshadowing teacher response. *College English, 60*(4), 374-395.

Wergin, J. F. (1988). Basic issues and principles in classroom assessment. In J. H. McMillan (Ed.), *Assessing students' learning* (pp. 5-17). New Directions for Teaching and Learning No. 34. San Francisco: Jossey-Bass.

Wiggins, G. (1998). *Educative assessment: Designing assessments to inform and improve student performance.* San Francisco: Jossey-Bass.

INDEX

A

achievement of course objectives, 35-57

achievement targets, kinds of, 10-13

achievement, ways to communicate, 69-71

analytic rubrics, 47-48

      content knowledge, 47

      thesis and organization, 47

      writing style and mechanics, 47

assessing students, purpose of, 1

assessment, 1-7

      as part of a model of instruction, 2-3

      classroom, 3

      definition of, 1

      educational, 3

      literature on, 5-6

      performance, 48-53

      professional standards for, 6-7

      student, 6-7

assessment in the disciplines, 59-68

      English/language arts, 60-62

      mathematics, 62-64

      natural sciences, 65-68

      social sciences, 64-65

assessment resources, 13-22

C

classroom assessment, 3

      in colleges and universities, 14-22

      options, 35-58

      quality of, 23-33

colleagues, getting ideas from, 94-95

combining individual scores into course grades, 75-82

      median, 76-77

      methods, 75-79

      total points, 77-79

      weighted letter grades, 79-80

course planning, 93

criterion referencing, 17-22

D

disciplines, assessment in, 59-68

Since 1983, the Association for the Study of Higher Education (ASHE) and the Educational Resources Information Center (ERIC) Clearinghouse on Higher Education, a sponsored project of the Graduate School of Education and Human Development at The George Washington University, have cosponsored the ASHE-ERIC Higher Education Report series. This volume is the twenty-seventh overall and the tenth to be published by the Graduate School of Education and Human Development at The George Washington University.

Each monograph is the definitive analysis of a tough higher education problem, based on thorough research of pertinent literature and institutional experiences. Topics are identified by a national survey. Noted practitioners and scholars are then commissioned to write the reports, with experts providing critical reviews of each manuscript before publication.

Eight monographs (10 before 1985) in the ASHE-ERIC Higher Education Report series are published each year and are available on individual and subscription bases. To order, use the order form on the last page of this book.

Qualified persons interested in writing a monograph for the ASHE-ERIC Higher Education Report series are invited to submit a proposal to the National Advisory Board. As the preeminent literature review and issue analysis series in higher education, the Higher Education Reports are guaranteed wide dissemination and national exposure for accepted candidates. Execution of a monograph requires at least a minimal familiarity with the ERIC database, including *Resources in Education* and the current *Index to Journals in Education*. The objective of these reports is to bridge conventional wisdom with practical research. Prospective authors are strongly encouraged to call at (800) 773-3742.

For further information, write to
    ASHE-ERIC Higher Education Report Series
    The George Washington University
    One Dupont Circle, Suite 630
    Washington, DC 20036-1183
Or phone (202) 296-2597
Toll free: (800) 773-ERIC

Write or call for a complete catalog.

Visit our Web site at **www.eriche.org/reports**

ADVISORY BOARD

James Earl Davis
University of Delaware at Newark

Kenneth A. Feldman
State University of New York–Stony Brook

Kassie Freeman
Peabody College, Vanderbilt University

Susan Frost
Emory University

Esther E. Gottlieb
West Virginia University

Philo Hutcheson
Georgia State University

Lori White
Stanford University

CONSULTING EDITORS

Sandra Beyer
University of Texas at El Paso

Robert Boice
State University of New York–Stony Brook

Ivy E. Broder
The American University

Dennis Brown
Michigan State University

Shirley M. Clark
Oregon State System of Higher Education

Robert A. Cornesky
Cornesky and Associates, Inc.

K. Patricia Cross
Scholar in Residence

Rhonda Martin Epper
State Higher Education Executive Officers

Anne H. Frank
American Association of University Professors

Mildred Garcia
Arizona State University–West

Don Hossler
Indiana University

Dean L. Hubbard
Northwest Missouri State University

Jean E. Hunter
Duquesne University

Lisa R. Lattuca
The Spencer Foundation, Chicago, Illinois

J. Roderick Lauver
Planned Systems International, Inc.–Maryland

Daniel T. Layzell
MGT of America, Inc., Madison, Wisconsin

Barbara Lee
Rutgers University

Robert Linn
University of Chicago

Ivan B. Liss
Radford University

Anne Goodsell Love
University of Akron

Clara M. Lovett
Northern Arizona University

Meredith Ludwig
Education Statistics Services Institute

Jean MacGregor
Evergreen State College

Laurence R. Marcus
Rowan College

William McKeachie
University of Michigan

Mantha V. Mehallis
Florida Atlantic University

Robert Menges
Northwestern University

Diane E. Morrison
Centre for Curriculum, Transfer, and Technology

Barbara M. Moskal
Colorado School of Mines

John A. Muffo
Virginia Polytechnic Institute and State University

Patricia H. Murrell
University of Memphis

L. Jackson Newell
Deep Springs College

Steven G. Olswang
University of Washington

R. Eugene Rice
American Association for Higher Education

Maria Scatena
St. Mary of the Woods College

John Schuh
Iowa State University

Jack H. Schuster
Claremont Graduate School–Center for Educational Studies

Carole Schwinn
Jackson Community College

Patricia Somers
University of Arkansas at Little Rock

Leonard Springer
University of Wisconsin–Madison

Richard J. Stiggins
Assessment and Training Institute

Marilla D. Svinicki
University of Texas–Austin

David Sweet
OERI, U.S. Department of Education

Catherine S. Taylor
University of Washington

Jon E. Travis
Texas A&M University

Dan W. Wheeler
University of Nebraska–Lincoln

Christine K. Wilkinson
Arizona State University

Donald H. Wulff
University of Washington

Manta Yorke
Liverpool John Moores University

William Zeller
University of Michigan at Ann Arbor

REVIEW PANEL

Richard Alfred
University of Michigan

Thomas A. Angelo
DePaul University

Charles Bantz
Arizona State University

Robert J. Barak
Iowa State Board of Regents

Alan Bayer
Virginia Polytechnic Institute and State University

John P. Bean
Indiana University–Bloomington

John M. Braxton
Peabody College, Vanderbilt University

Ellen M. Brier
Tennessee State University

Dennis Brown
University of Kansas

Deborah Faye Carter
Indiana University

Patricia Carter
University of Michigan

John A. Centra
Syracuse University

Paul B. Chewning
Council for the Advancement and Support of Education

Arthur W. Chickering
Vermont College

Darrel A. Clowes
Virginia Polytechnic Institute and State University

Carol L. Colbeck
Pennsylvania State University

Deborah M. DiCroce
Tidewater Virginia Community College

Marty Finkelstein
Seton Hall University

Dorothy E. Finnegan
The College of William & Mary

Timothy Gallineau
Buffalo State College

Judith Glazer-Raymo
Long Island University

Kenneth C. Green
Claremont Graduate University

James C. Hearn
University of Minnesota

Donald E. Heller
University of Michigan

Edward R. Hines
Illinois State University

Deborah Hirsch
University of Massachusetts

Deborah Hunter
University of Vermont

Linda K. Johnsrud
University of Hawaii at Manoa

Bruce Anthony Jones
University of Missouri–Columbia

Elizabeth A. Jones
West Virginia University

Marsha V. Krotseng
Cleveland State University

George D. Kuh
Indiana University–Bloomington

J. Roderick Lauver
Planned Systems International, Inc.–Maryland

Daniel T. Layzell
MGT of America, Inc., Madison, Wisconsin

Ronald Lee
University of Nebraska

Patrick G. Love
Kent State University

Mantha V. Mehallis
Florida Atlantic University

Marcia Mentkowski
Alverno College

John Milam, Jr.
George Mason University

Toby Milton
Essex Community College

Christopher C. Morphew
University of Kansas

John A. Muffo
Virginia Polytechnic Institute and State University

L. Jackson Newell
Deep Springs College

Mark Oromaner
Hudson County Community College

Suzanne Ortega
University of Nebraska

James C. Palmer
Illinois State University

Michael Paulson
University of New Orleans

Robert A. Rhoads
Michigan State University

G. Jeremiah Ryan
Quincy College

Mary Ann Danowitz Sagaria
The Ohio State University

Kathleen M. Shaw
Temple University

Edward St. John
Indiana University

Scott Swail
College Bound

J. Douglas Toma
University of Missouri–Kansas City

Kathryn Nemeth Tuttle
University of Kansas

David S. Webster
Oklahoma State University

Lisa Wolf
University of Kansas

Volume 26 ASHE-ERIC Higher Education Reports

1. Faculty Workload Studies: Perspectives, Needs, and Future Directions
   Katrina A. Meyer

2. Assessing Faculty Publication Productivity: Issues of Equity
   Elizabeth G. Creamer

3. Proclaiming and Sustaining Excellence: Assessment as a Faculty Role
   Karen Maitland Schilling and Karl L. Schilling

4. Creating Learning Centered Classrooms: What Does Learning Theory Have to Say?
   Frances K. Stage, Patricia A. Muller, Jillian Kinzie, and Ada Simmons

5. The Academic Administrator and the Law: What Every Dean and Department Chair Needs to Know
   J. Douglas Toma and Richard L. Palm

6. The Powerful Potential of Learning Communities: Improving Education for the Future
   Oscar T. Lenning and Larry H. Ebbers

7. Enrollment Management for the 21st Century: Institutional Goals, Accountability, and Fiscal Responsibility
   Garlene Penn

8. Enacting Diverse Learning Environments: Improving the Climate for Racial/Ethnic Diversity in Higher Education
   Sylvia Hurtado, Jeffrey Milem, Alma Clayton-Pedersen, and Walter Allen

Volume 25 ASHE-ERIC Higher Education Reports

1. A Culture for Academic Excellence: Implementing the Quality Principles in Higher Education
   Jann E. Freed, Marie R. Klugman, and Jonathan D. Fife

2. From Discipline to Development: Rethinking Student Conduct in Higher Education
   Michael Dannells

3. Academic Controversy: Enriching College Instruction Through Intellectual Conflict
   David W. Johnson, Roger T. Johnson, and Karl A. Smith

4. Higher Education Leadership: Analyzing the Gender Gap
   Luba Chliwniak

5. The Virtual Campus: Technology and Reform in Higher Education
   Gerald C. Van Dusen

6. Early Intervention Programs: Opening the Door to Higher Education
   Robert H. Fenske, Christine A. Geranios, Jonathan E. Keller, and David E. Moore

7. The Vitality of Senior Faculty Members: Snow on the Roof— Fire in the Furnace
   Carole J. Bland and William H. Bergquist

8. A National Review of Scholastic Achievement in General Education: How Are We Doing and Why Should We Care?
   Steven J. Osterlind

Volume 24 ASHE-ERIC Higher Education Reports

1. Tenure, Promotion, and Reappointment: Legal and Administrative Implications
   Benjamin Baez and John A. Centra

2. Taking Teaching Seriously: Meeting the Challenge of Instructional Improvement
   Michael B. Paulsen and Kenneth A. Feldman

3. Empowering the Faculty: Mentoring Redirected and Renewed
   Gaye Luna and Deborah L. Cullen

4. Enhancing Student Learning: Intellectual, Social, and Emotional Integration
   Anne Goodsell Love and Patrick G. Love

5. Benchmarking in Higher Education: Adapting Best Practices to Improve Quality
   Jeffrey W. Alstete

6. Models for Improving College Teaching: A Faculty Resource
   Jon E. Travis

7. Experiential Learning in Higher Education: Linking Classroom and Community
   Jeffrey A. Cantor

8. Successful Faculty Development and Evaluation: The Complete Teaching Portfolio
   John P. Murray

Volume 23 ASHE-ERIC Higher Education Reports

1. The Advisory Committee Advantage: Creating an Effective Strategy for Programmatic Improvement
   Lee Teitel

2. Collaborative Peer Review: The Role of Faculty in Improving College Teaching
   Larry Keig and Michael D. Waggoner

3. Prices, Productivity, and Investment: Assessing Financial Strategies in Higher Education
   Edward P. St. John

4. The Development Officer in Higher Education: Toward an Understanding of the Role
   Michael J. Worth and James W. Asp II

5. Measuring Up: The Promises and Pitfalls of Performance Indicators in Higher Education
   Gerald Gaither, Brian P. Nedwek, and John E. Neal

6. A New Alliance: Continuous Quality and Classroom Effectiveness
   Mimi Wolverton

7. Redesigning Higher Education: Producing Dramatic Gains in Student Learning
   Lion F. Gardiner

8. Student Learning Outside the Classroom: Transcending Artificial Boundaries
   George D. Kuh, Katie Branch Douglas, Jon P. Lund, and Jackie Ramin-Gyurnek

Volume 22 ASHE-ERIC Higher Education Reports

1. The Department Chair: New Roles, Responsibilities, and Challenges
   Alan T. Seagren, John W. Creswell, and Daniel W. Wheeler

2. Sexual Harassment in Higher Education: From Conflict to Community
   Robert O. Riggs, Patricia H. Murrell, and JoAnne C. Cutting

3. Chicanos in Higher Education: Issues and Dilemmas for the 21st Century
   Adalberto Aguirre, Jr., and Ruben O. Martinez

4. Academic Freedom in American Higher Education: Rights, Responsibilities, and Limitations
   Robert K. Poch

5. Making Sense of the Dollars: The Costs and Uses of Faculty Compensation
   Kathryn M. Moore and Marilyn J. Amey

6. Enhancing Promotion, Tenure, and Beyond: Faculty Socialization as a Cultural Process
   William G. Tierney and Robert A. Rhoads

7. New Perspectives for Student Affairs Professionals: Evolving Realities, Responsibilities, and Roles
   Peter H. Garland and Thomas W. Grace

8. Turning Teaching Into Learning: The Role of Student Responsibility in the Collegiate Experience
   Todd M. Davis and Patricia Hillman Murrell

Quantity   **Amount**

_____ Please begin my subscription to the current year's
ASHE-ERIC Higher Education Reports at $144.00, over
25% off the cover price, starting with Report 1.   _____

_____ Please send a complete set of Volume _____
ASHE-ERIC Higher Education Reports at $144.00, over
25% off the cover price.   _____

Individual reports are available for $24.00 and include the cost of shipping and handling.

SECURE ON-LINE ORDERING
is now available on our web site.
www.eriche.org/reports

SHIPPING POLICY:

• Books are sent UPS Ground or equivalent. For faster delivery, call for charges. Alaska, Hawaii, U.S. Territories, and Foreign Countries, please call for shipping information. Order will be shipped within 24 hours after receipt of request. Orders of 10 or more books, call for shipping information. All prices shown are subject to change.

• Returns: No cash refunds—credit will be applied to future orders.

PLEASE SEND ME THE FOLLOWING REPORTS:

Quantity	Volume/No.	Title	Amount

Please check one of the following:
☐ Check enclosed, payable to GW-ERIC.
☐ Purchase order attached.
☐ Charge my credit card indicated below:
   ☐ Visa   ☐ MasterCard

Subtotal: _____

Less Discount: _____

Total Due: _____

Expiration Date_____

Name_____

Title _____ E-mail _____

Institution _____

Address_____

City _____ State _____ Zip_____

Phone _____ Fax _____Telex_____

Signature _____ Date_____

SEND ALL ORDERS TO:
ASHE-ERIC Higher Education Reports Series
One Dupont Cir., Ste. 630, Washington, DC 20036-1183
Phone: (202) 296-2597 ext. 13 Toll-free: (800) 773-ERIC ext. 13
FAX: (202) 452-1844
EMAIL: order@eric-he.edu
Secure on-line ordering at URL: www.eriche.org/reports

**Secure on-line ordering
is available:
visit our Web site at
www.eriche.org/reports**